The Demographic Dividend and the Power of Youth

The Demographic Dividend and the Power of Youth

Voices from the Global Diplomacy Lab

Edited by

Eirliani Abdul Rahman, ElsaMarie D'Silva
and Sonja Peteranderl

ANTHEM PRESS

Anthem Press
An imprint of Wimbledon Publishing Company
www.anthempress.com

This edition first published in UK and USA 2021
by ANTHEM PRESS
75–76 Blackfriars Road, London SE1 8HA, UK
or PO Box 9779, London SW19 7ZG, UK
and
244 Madison Ave #116, New York, NY 10016, USA

Global Diplomacy Lab

British Library Cataloguing-in-Publication Data
A catalogue record for this book is available from the British Library.

Library of Congress Control Number: 2021930105

ISBN-13: 978-1-78527-631-6 (Hbk)
ISBN-10: 1-78527-631-X (Hbk)

Cover image: Photograph by Sonja Peteranderl

This title is also available as an e-book.

CONTENTS

ILLUSTRATIONS

Figures

Tables

FOREWORD

Reinventing Diplomacy

Thirty years after the fall of the Berlin Wall, our world has changed dramatically. We are not experiencing the 'end of history', as some analysts have forecasted, but our societies are going through a phase of great uncertainty and turmoil.

The speed of digital advancement in all areas of life reflects an enormous leap in technological innovation, opening the door for new opportunities. But it has, at the same time, been an unprecedented engine for globalisation – a source of great insecurity for many people who feel increasingly powerless in an ever more complex world. People are longing for simple answers to complex problems, which leaders are unable to provide. Rising frustration, withdrawal into the private, resurgence of nationalist trends and radicalisation of opinions are resulting phenomena. We see a loss of common sense, of solidarity in many of our societies, and an erosion of our very value system which has been the guarantor for freedom, stability and prosperity in the past two generations.

These domestic trends are mirrored in international relations. The system of global governance is rapidly eroding. It must be a major concern if multilateral organisations and treaties are deconstructed by the architect of this system, if 'America First' is putting transatlantic partnerships in question and if a rising power like China is starting to fill the vacuum created by interest-driven national concepts of governance. Autocratic leaders are en vogue, propaganda is replacing dialogue and national interest is pushing aside action to defend global common goods.

Despite all deficiencies, the existing global system has been a framework for driving positive development in many regions over seven decades. Notwithstanding, 75 years after the creation of the United Nations, it needs more than an overhaul. It needs a complete renovation to make it fit for the twenty-first century.

Europe, which is the most successful prototype of supranational cooperation, would be a perfect leader in the process of modernising the international system. But the European Union is weakened by populism and other domestic developments at a time when it is direly needed as a bridge-builder. In Europe and elsewhere, this sober assessment requires new thinking and new concepts of action.

What is needed more than ever is responsible leadership. Governments alone are no longer capable of solving the complex challenges we face. What is of the essence now is cooperation between all stakeholders in society – politics, business, science, culture, civic society.

It is indispensable that responsible leaders from all sectors and regions in the world pool their experience, creativity and influence to build a new community of purpose – a community driven by the conviction that the implementation of the 2030 Agenda of the United Nations is not an option but a duty; that the fulfillment of the obligations under the Paris Agreement is not a quantité négligeable but the precondition for preventing climate change from becoming irreversible; a leadership which does not misuse a pandemic to stir conflicts with equally affected societies, but instead engages in cross-sectoral and cross-regional cooperation to build a network of solidary action. The COVID-19 challenge we are still facing in all societies is a blunt but maybe necessary wake-up call for leaders in all societies.

The key to making a difference is trust. Trust between leaders at all levels of society. This has been the very rationale for an initiative which has been a co-creation between the German Foreign Office, the BMW Foundation, the Bosch Foundation and the Mercator Foundation: the Global Diplomacy Lab (GDL).

The GDL, emerging from the Africa Lab on the continent's potential of the demographic dividend, introduced a process of communication and action already in its first five years of existence that can be regarded as an added value to traditional diplomacy. The Lab, which invites creative entrepreneurs, artists, journalists, academics and diplomats, is much more than a series of conferences addressing the future of foreign policy.

It has grown into an innovative platform, bringing together a diversity of viewpoints, disciplines, and sectors, creating a safe space for freewheeling ideas, for listening to the unexpected or even the challenging and for building trust between people with entirely different backgrounds.

Contrary to traditional diplomacy, priority is not the What, it is the How. It is not aiming at quick solutions in the shortest possible delay, but rather building a framework for personal respect, for inspiring each other, for playing with ideas – a laboratory in the best sense.

When a graphic designer from Asia, a human rights lawyer from Latin America, a criminologist from Scandinavia, a journalist from Chicago and a diplomat from South Africa tackle the question 'How can we better prevent mass atrocities?' in the GDL's Open Situation Room, no idea is too absurd or far-fetched. Ideas pile in, some related to strengthening the political will, some to new ways of collaboration between organisations in Africa and Latin America. Sometimes people who are not so familiar with the topic provide the best input.

The GDL is about breaking down a highly structured environment, inviting new and unlikely actors to challenge protocol and traditional thinking, looking for new ways to tackle the complex problems of the twenty-first century. Listening to each other, understanding the often very different mindset of the other and daring to leave one's own silo are processes which create opportunities of cooperation between politics and business, business and civil society, civic organisations and governmental agencies.

Entering a dialogue at eye level and without respect for formal levels of decision-making power opens doors to address situations proactively which could otherwise evolve into open conflict.

Forty years ago, I had the honour of pushing an initiative in the Legal Committee of the UN General Assembly together with representatives from Japan, Italy, India and Brazil. We rightly concentrated on pre-empting possible conflicts, as action to tackle hot conflicts were already then condemned to failure, due to the veto of the five Permanent Members in the UN Security Council. This initiative became the famous Agenda for Peace by late UN Secretary-General Perez de Cuellar. It had the right intention, but the wrong concept. Its deficiency was the traditional focus on governments and international organisations as sole actors of conflict prevention, peacekeeping, peacemaking and peacebuilding.

The GDL approach, including all relevant actors of society in this complex process of restoring and building peace, is as innovative as it is warranted.

I congratulate all participants of the GDL over the past years, the team which has been very successful in developing this innovative concept, guided by Ruprecht Polenz and our partners supporting this process. You have inspired an amazing co-creation of people who have taken ownership and risk to put on track an example which I hope will inspire many other diplomatic communities around the globe. Your motivation and political will stand in stark contrast to the sometimes gloomy picture of global affairs.

Make it a sustainable effort and you will make a significant contribution to finding creative answers to the challenges ahead.

HE Dr. Michael Schaefer
Ambassador
Chairman, BMW Foundation Herbert Quandt

NOTES ON CONTRIBUTORS

Editors

Eirliani Abdul Rahman, FRSA, is an award-winning author and child rights activist. Her book *Survivors: Breaking the Silence on Child Sexual Abuse* was published in 2017 and is now in its third print run. She contributed a case study to the medical textbook *Essentials of Global Health*, published by Elsevier in London in 2018. The book won the first prize under the Public Health category in the 2019 British Medical Association book awards. In 2015, she won the BMW Foundation Responsible Leaders Award for her work on child sexual abuse and child sex trafficking. Eirliani is programme director for Nobel Peace laureate Kailash Satyarthi's NGO in the United States and global COO and board member of Red Dot Foundation Global. Her work has been featured in the media in the United States and the Asia Pacific and in the *Sunday Times* in the United Kingdom. She served as a diplomat in the Singapore Foreign Service for 10 years. Eirliani is a fellow of the London-based Royal Society for the Encouragement of Arts, Manufactures and Commerce and holds an MSc in public administration and public policy from the London School of Economics. Twitter: @eirliani.

ElsaMarie D'Silva is the founder and CEO of Red Dot Foundation (India) and president of Red Dot Foundation Global (United States). She is a gender equality advocate, activist and social entrepreneur. She is also a 2019 Reagan Fascell Fellow, a 2018 Yale World Fellow and an alumni of the Stanford Draper Hills Summer School, the US State Department's Fortune Mentoring Program, Oxford Chevening Gurukul and the Duke of Edinburgh's Commonwealth Leadership Program. ElsaMarie is a fellow with Rotary Peace, Aspen New Voices and Vital Voices and a BMW Foundation Responsible Leader. She lives in Mumbai, India, and loves to sugarcraft when not writing articles or evangelising gender equality around the world.

Sonja Peteranderl is a Latin America correspondent for *Der Spiegel* in Tijuana, Mexico, and founder of BuzzingCities Lab, a think tank focusing on how digitalisation influences security, organised crime and urban violence in megacities. She covers technology, security/policing, organised crime/cyber-crime, migration and social justice. Previously, she served as a technology editor at *Der Spiegel* and senior editor for *Wired Germany Magazine* and spent a decade as a freelance foreign correspondent for media such as *Der Spiegel*, *Zeit Online*, *Süddeutsche Zeitung*, *Tagesspiegel* and *Impulse*. She is a Kellen fellow at the American Council on Germany researching the impact of algorithms in the policing/security realm and a member of the Global Diplomacy Lab (GDL) and the Bosch Alumni Network. Twitter: @glocalreporting.

Contributing Authors

Stefan Cibian is the executive director and co-founder of the Făgăraș Research Institute. He is an academy associate with Chatham House – The Royal Institute of International Affairs, Africa Programme. He also teaches courses related to international development at Babeș-Bolyai University, focusing on development and statehood in Sub-Saharan Africa, CEE and EU-Africa relations, development policy, international relations theory, peacebuilding, democratisation, civil society and philanthropy, migration and human rights. Stefan is the president of FOND, the Romanian NGDO Platform, and GRASP (Global Romanian Society of Young Professionals) and the treasurer of CONCORD, the European NGO Confederation for Humanitarian Aid and Development. He is also a board member at Țara Făgărașului Community Foundation (FCTF), the Romanian Federation of Community Foundations (FFCR), the Romanian Association for International Cooperation and Development (ARCADIA) and UiPath Foundation.

Rudrani Dasgupta is a researcher, mentor and peacebuilder. Her work focuses on young people and children's rights. She is the co-founder of Chai Ki Dukaan, a digital Track II diplomacy peace platform for friendly dialogue between Indians and Pakistanis. She presented her work on this platform to the international community at the UN High Level Political Forum Meeting in 2019 at the UN Headquarters. A member of the Global Leadership Academy under the aegis of the German technical cooperation agency GIZ, Rudrani is also an active member of the Global Diplomacy Lab and the GLAC-Thomson Reuters Lab on Trafficking in Persons. Currently, she is with ActionAid India as a programme officer. A University College London alumnus, Rudrani is a published author writing on youth, identity and higher education for academic and media publications such as the *International Journal for Children's Rights (Brill)*, *Times Higher Education* and *The Wire*.

Lynn Houmdi is a published author and genuine expert on all things Swiri (i.e. Essaouiran), having lived in the bohemian fishing town on Morocco's Atlantic Coast for a number of years. In 2018, she conducted an ethnographic study of the town's unemployed graduates for her master's in Islamic and Middle Eastern studies, for which she received a prize from the University of Edinburgh. With her Swiri husband and their son, Lynn divides her time between Essaouira and Edinburgh, Scotland. As well as writing and consulting for various clients with an interest in Morocco, she supports non-profits and small businesses to grow and communicate with purpose. Lynn has developed several projects with the Challenges Group, a family of consultancies providing enterprising solutions to global challenges (https://thechallengesgroup.com/), about whose work she has written in this volume. You can find more writing by Lynn on her blog maroc-o-phile.com. Twitter: https://twitter.com/maroc_o_phile.

Kebba-Omar Jagne is the founder of Making Our Visions and Aspirations Reality (MOVAAR) group, an educational technology scale-up and a Civicus Alliance member. He holds an MSc in science, technology and innovation (STI) studies from the University of Sussex, United Kingdom, and a bachelor's degree in economics/political science from Hofstra University, United States. He has served his native Gambia through the United Nations and the US Department of State and also completed several international fellowships in STI and economics. Omar is a member of the Global Diplomacy Lab (GDL) and is based in the Gambia.

Julia Jaroschewski is an investigative journalist, political scientist (MA) and the founder of BuzzingCities Lab, a think tank that investigates how digitalisation affects security and criminal organisations in hotspots of urban violence such as favelas in Brazil. She is also a lecturer on security and drug policy. Julia studied political science, sociology and communication sciences at the Free University of Berlin and the Universidade de Coimbra. As a freelance foreign correspondent, she has reported from Latin America, the United States, India and Africa for media such as *Der Spiegel*, *Wired Germany Magazine* and *Die Welt* over the past 10 years, focusing on foreign politics, organised crime/drug war and security policy. As a fellow of the German Academic Scholarship Foundation and the Dr Rita and Alexander Besser Foundation, she reported from Brazil and South Africa. Julia is a member of the Global Diplomacy Lab (GDL) and the Bosch Alumni network.

Elizabeth Maloba is a moderator, speaker and entrepreneur. She has 20 years of experience in addressing complex challenges. She works in cross-sectoral, trans-professional, multi-stakeholder settings to enable people to make decisions, solve problems, exchange ideas and information and learn. Elizabeth is highly experienced in international cooperation, development cooperation and private sector development. She works in cross-cultural groups, from the grassroots level to global platforms, to support development of leaders, teams, policies, strategies, plans and business models that contribute to addressing development challenges. She brings skills in capacity building, knowledge management, facilitation, conflict resolution and management as well as experience as an entrepreneur to diverse assignments. Elizabeth lives in Nairobi, works across the world and speaks English, Swahili, German and French.

Colette Mazzucelli is senior vice president (Academia) at the Global Listening Centre (https://www.globallisteningcentre.org/global-listening-board/academia/) and has taught since 2004 on graduate faculty in international relations and global affairs across schools, GSAS and SPS, at NYU New York. She is editor with James Felton Keith of the Anthem Press Ethics of Personal Data Collection Series. As a member of the Global Diplomacy Lab (GDL) and a BMW Foundation Responsible Leader, Colette also serves on the International Advisory Board of The Data Union. At Long Island's University Global and Pioneer Academics, she teaches international relations (conflict resolution/Europe) reaching students on six continents through her design of experiential, innovative, technology-mediated seminars. Since 1993, Colette's biography has appeared in numerous *Marquis Who's Who* publications, notably *Marquis Who's Who in America* and *Marquis Who's Who in the World.*

Patrick Mpedzisi is an organisational development consultant with 19 years of experience in the development sector. Previously, he was the coordinator of the African Youth Parliament (2003–2007) where he worked on continental youth processes while engaging with the African Union (AU). He continued working closely with the AU and its structures as coordinator of the African Democracy Forum and project coordinator at the Southern Africa Trust. Patrick studied law at the University of Zimbabwe. He is the secretary general for the Zimbabwe Evaluation Association, a BMW Responsible Leader and a member of the Bosch Alumni Network and the Global Leadership Academy (GLAC).

Viola Prisca Roggia is a graduate candidate at New York University. She is working on an MS degree in global affairs, focusing on transnational security and specialising in data analytics. During her graduate studies, she worked for the United Nations in New York and the National Consortium for the Study of Terrorism and Responses to Terrorism in Maryland, conducting research on terrorism and hate crimes. Viola has a background in economics, having earned a BA in economics from the University of Trento, and has worked for the Chamber of Commerce in Bolzano.

Christian Rossi is associate professor of history of international relations at the Department of Political and Social Sciences, University of Cagliari, Italy, where he teaches history of European integration for the bachelor's course on political science and European integration for the master's course on international relations. Since 2018, he is deputy director of the Department of Political and Social Sciences. Christian's research interests vary from British foreign politics to Mediterranean politics and to the history of the European Union and integration. His publications include: 'China 2017: Searching for Internal and International Consent', *Asia Maior*, 28 (2018); and 'The Ideas of a European Entity in the International Relations between the XIX and the First Half of XX Century', in Gilbert Gornig and Christina Bohle (eds), *Nation – Nationalität – Staat: Nation – Nationality – State*, vol. 1, pp. 59–70 (Klages-Verlag, 2013).

Annegret Warth is an educational scientist, active at the intersection of research and policymaking. Her research interests are international youth research and international youth policy development. In the past 10 years, she has been active in the field of youth exchanges and international youth policy cooperation with a focus on Germany and Turkey. For her PhD, Annegret is researching heterogeneous youth in Turkey and developing a heuristic concept of youth that aims to include youth realities beyond western European countries. As a 2018–19 Mercator-IPC Fellow, she initiated a multi-stakeholder discourse on local youth policy development in Turkey. Annegret studied at Tübingen University and Bosphorus University in Istanbul and holds a diploma in educational sciences from Marburg University, Germany.

Ekua Yankah, PhD, MPH, is an Afro-German social scientist, activist and social entrepreneur. She received her doctorate in social epidemiology from the London School of Hygiene & Tropical Medicine, University of London. For the past 20 years, she has worked as a staff member and senior consultant for various United Nations agencies, international NGOs and academic institutions in Southeast Asia, Sub-Saharan Africa and Europe. Ekua recently joined the Berlin-based femtech start-up 'Clue'.

INTRODUCTION

Eirliani Abdul Rahman, ElsaMarie D'Silva
and Sonja Peteranderl

In India, the youth learn how to design interventions in their own neighbourhoods to combat sexual violence, and in Brazil, young people from favelas use technology to document police violence and disseminate their perspectives on the social and political situation in their country.

All over the world, the youth are key to a society in fostering not only positive social, political and cultural changes but economic change as well. A variety of approaches and tools try to harness the potential of young people – often without considering their real needs and without empowering them to bring about change themselves. This compendium of essays explores the role young people can play as actors of change and how international governments and institutions can effectively manage and take advantage of the demographic dividend.

'Demographic dividend' is a term coined by Harvard economists David Bloom and David Canning to represent the boost in economic growth that can result from changes in a country's population age structure. As fertility rates decrease, a country's working-age population grows larger relative to the young dependent population. With more people in the labour force and fewer children to support, a country has a window of opportunity for rapid economic growth if the right social and economic investments and policies are made in health, education, governance and the economy. Conversely, research shows that resource requirements to support a large population of children and youth can depress the pace of economic growth and prevent needed investments in human capital.

The discourse on responding to this population growth frequently excludes the youth. The result can be an apathetic community of young people who withdraw from participation in political and democratic processes. In their chapters for this collection, members of the Global Diplomacy Lab (GDL) as well as associated experts from various continents address the issue and highlight solutions from different parts of the world and thus provide transferable approaches to promote, enhance and contribute to harvesting the demographic dividend.

The GDL is a think-do tank founded in Berlin to turn diplomacy on its head by involving non-state and non-traditional actors and utilising non-traditional methodologies for framing discussions. There is a need to systematically make diplomacy more inclusive and open what was previously a comparably closed realm of career diplomats, policymakers and academic think tanks to deepen exchange, innovation and co-creation with other actors. All involved in traditional and non-traditional diplomacy face the need to enhance their capacities to coordinate, collaborate and leverage each other's strengths in dealing with global challenges.

The GDL has the ambition to realise inclusive and transformative diplomacy. We call this Diplomacy 4.0. We strive to play a part in establishing a global system that is characterised by mutual accountability, respect and inclusiveness, and which delivers positive transformational change. This is done through innovative and collaborative formats in a wide variety of activities to explore new tools of communication based on mutual trust and reformulate an agenda for collective action. Every year, the GDL hosts labs to solve a real-life challenge put forward by a partner and agreed upon by the members. The GDL itself is a unique set-up: a public-private partnership wherein the German Federal Foreign Office partners with private foundations to push for a more inclusive diplomacy. It is supported by the German Federal Foreign Office, the BMW Foundation Herbert Quandt, the Robert Bosch Stiftung, the Stiftung Mercator, Fulbright Germany and The Global Leadership Academy of the German technical cooperation agency, the GIZ.

In 2019, the theme of the labs in Ghana and Germany was 'Global Power Shifts: Political and Economic Inclusion for the Next Generation Collaborating to Realise the Potential of the Demographic Dividend' and the challenge holder was the German Federal Foreign Office. This compendium seeks to build on some of the ideas discussed during the lab and highlight the work of some of the members, their organisations and associated experts. In fact, it was a direct output from the lab so that there could be more material and concrete ideas on the topic.

As such, it is not our aim in this compendium to provide a comprehensive literature review. We are interested in a particular form of story-telling, of documenting the processes that are co-created and collaborative and involve non-state and non-traditional actors. In seeking out the stories and best practices, we are looking for unique perspectives on how work in one's field seeks to promote, or has promoted, human dignity. The diverse approaches presented and analysed in this collection range from local entrepreneurial initiatives or activism to state-funded public programmes to technological innovation. Our approach is thus oriented towards problem-solving and less focused on theory while bringing our collective experiences into the conversation. We want to make such work accessible, especially to young people, and bridge the gap between theory and practice. This compendium of essays is targeted at development practitioners, policymakers and students pursuing undergraduate and postgraduate studies in international development and/or global studies.

In her chapter 'Reaping Morocco's Demographic Dividend: Lessons from Sub-Saharan Africa', Lynn Houmdi analyses, for example, how the Challenges Group manages to tackle youth unemployment in sub-Saharan Africa. The coalition of non-profits, social enterprise and impact businesses departs from the usual model of grant-aided development assistance and brings together communities to grow economies sustainably and in a participatory manner from the bottom up.

Ekua Yankah demonstrates in the chapter 'Putting the African Girl at the Centre of Demographic Change Programmes' how African countries have navigated their demographic transitions with programmes that put the needs of girls front and centre.

Rudrani Dasgupta examines the role of mental well-being. With over one-fifth of its population being between 15 and 24 years of age, India is the 'youngest country' in the world – and according to the World Health Organization (WHO), also the most depressed nation. In her chapter 'Digital Mindfulness for Indian Millennials', Dasgupta shows how millennials are using meditation and mindfulness apps to cope with emerging mental health issues such as depression and anxiety in a society with limited access to affordable mental health care.

Technology can empower young people, but it is not the final solution to structural problems. Government programmes can bring about structural change but will not be successful without the participation and commitment of young people who themselves help shape change. In this book, we want to identify ways to increase inclusion, ownership and sustainability, foster a shared global understanding of the challenge and present different approaches and actors that need to work together to harvest the demographic dividend.

March 2020

Description of the cover image

In South Los Angeles, a disadvantaged, violence ridden part of Los Angeles in the United States, black and brown youth are often deprived of education and job opportunities. For many, Nipsey Hussle became a symbol of a different future: He grew up in the gang world, but became a successful rapper. Throughout his career, he tried to unite the rival gang members from Los Angeles with music projects and was committed to the economic development of the neighbourhood. On March 31, 2019, Nipsey became a victim of the violence himself and was shot dead. Today, at the scene of the crime, graffiti commemorates the rapper – and he continues to inspire the young generation to contribute to positive change.

Chapter 1

REAPING MOROCCO'S DEMOGRAPHIC DIVIDEND: LESSONS FROM SUB-SAHARAN AFRICA

Lynn Houmdi

Ten years after the protests of the 20 February Movement, Morocco's 'Arab Spring' moment, demonstrations still take place almost daily across the kingdom on a range of issues.[1] From the unemployed graduates to the miners of Jerada, from the contractual teachers to the Soulaliyate women demanding land rights, from the Mediterranean to the Sahara, social unrest is largely driven by a lack of social justice and/or secure economic opportunities (Rachidi, 2019).

Across North Africa, the youth demographic is the widest and yet the most economically excluded. According to the International Labour Organisation (ILO, 2017), 'Reduced economic activity rates (youth leaving or postponing their entry into the labour market), under-employment (working below one's qualifications or fewer hours than one would wish to), increased precarity and informal work are [...] dominant characteristics of the lives at work of North Africa's youth.' Furthermore, the better educated a Moroccan job seeker is, the more likely s/he is to be unemployed (Chraibi, 2019).[2] Graduate unemployment has hovered around 25–30 per cent for decades across North Africa (World Bank, n.d., 'Fact Sheet'). The availability of public sector jobs-for-life

---

My thanks to Stephen Hunt, research manager at the Challenges Group, for his input to, and suggestions for, this chapter. Information about the work of the Challenges Group has been sourced from public and internal documents. For more information on the work of the group, see: https://thechallengesgroup.com/.

1 This chapter was written before the COVID-19 global pandemic; the resultant economic slowdown will have a significant impact on Morocco's ability to implement the measures suggested, although they are likely to be more pressing than ever.

2 Economic and population statistics are available on the website of the Moroccan Haut Commissariat au Plan (HCP): https://www.hcp.ma.

which absorbed the graduates of previous generations is much reduced in a contracted, neoliberal state, yet the knowledge and skills acquired in Morocco's state universities are not relevant in an increasingly globalised marketplace. According to the International Monetary Fund (IMF, 2016, p. 13), 'Education quality and skill mismatches are widely recognized as impediments to the youth population gaining a foothold in the labour market.'

A 2017 joint report by Morocco's High Commission for Planning (Haut Commissariat de Plan; HCP) in collaboration with the World Bank, entitled 'Labour Market in Morocco: Challenges and Opportunities', highlighted three challenges preventing Morocco from harvesting its demographic dividend. These were: (1) a lack of inclusion, (2) slow job creation and (3) the low quality of jobs. Taking each of the three areas highlighted by the HCP/World Bank report in turn, this chapter highlights a number of case studies of practical and successful initiatives which have been undertaken in sub-Saharan economies and which could be adapted to the Moroccan situation to help reap a demographic dividend and avoid the consequences of a dividend left to wither on the vine, to continue the agricultural analogy.

Labour Market in Morocco: Challenges and Opportunities

Morocco's demographic transition began in 1980 and is set to tail off by 2025 (Harkat and Driouchi, 2017, p. 6).

> The demographic bonus or demographic dividend refers to the opportunity created over a period of about 40–50 years during which, as a result of reduced proportions of dependent children, the proportion of the population of labour force age increases significantly, resulting in direct and indirect opportunities to increase per capita output. (Sathar et al., 2013, p. 5)

Morocco's dependency ratio, that is, the ratio of dependents to the active labour force, peaked at 105 per cent in 1967, just over a decade after independence. By 2018, it had halved (World Bank, 2019a). The gap between birth and mortality rates has become narrower over time (Dufrénot, 2018, p. 5), although it is currently stagnating (Youssef et al., 2018, p. 2). The growth in the working-age population as a proportion of the total population – currently larger than children and elderly combined – represents Morocco's demographic potential, but the window of opportunity to reap this demographic dividend is closing.

Bloom et al. (2017, pp. 70–71) outline a combination of investment in social capital, including measures to improve access to education and female participation in the workforce, and policy measures designed to accumulate physical capital and human capital which would be necessary to reap the benefits of the demographic dividend. The United Nations Population Fund (2017) underlines the potential for adequate social policies to support 'more savings in households and better living standards'. The 2013 Cairo Declaration of the Regional Conference on Population and Development in the Arab States also highlighted the need for strategic interventions such as 'legislations, policies and programmes and training' to ensure that young people delivered on the dividend.

The demographic dividend can be realised only when demographic transition is accompanied by economic transition. Active labour market policies (ALMPs) need to combine supply-side and demand-side measures (ILO, 2017, p. 29) alongside macroeconomic policies to achieve a structural transformation of the economy. The World Bank (2015, p. 3) notes that 'one of the key challenges for Morocco is that economic growth has not achieved enough employment growth to the needs of a saturated labour market', estimating the requirement of annual growth rates of 6–7 per cent to absorb new entrants into the labour market. Morocco is on an upward trajectory in terms of the ease of doing business, ranking 53rd of 190 economies in the World Bank Doing Business Report 2020 (World Bank, 2019b, pp. 84–85), but the GDP growth has not reached 6 per cent since 2005 and is currently around half of the World Bank's predicted requirement (World Bank, 2018a).

In order to secure inclusion alongside growth, the pace of the transition in Morocco is critical. The so-called youth bulge can be seen as a demographic gift of great potential, and young people are often framed as 'engines of growth, as the source of innovation and productivity' (World Bank, 2012). However, without appropriate structural interventions, there is a danger that the opportunity is missed, the transition mismanaged. This potentially means an even greater unproductive population without a social safety net as the bulge ages, rather than the positive impacts of tax revenue, increased spending and economic growth. In short, the dividend risks being substituted by economic stagnation (Mason et al., 2017, p. 1).

According to the World Bank, young people account for 60 per cent of Africa's unemployed. With 200 million people aged between 15 and 24, Africa has the largest population of young people in the world (Ighobor, 2017). Despite a GDP above the sub-Saharan African average (World Bank, 2018b), Morocco shares with its neighbours across Africa the problem of high youth, especially graduate, unemployment.

There is much to be learned between the north and the south on the African continent. The following sections of this chapter introduce Challenges and their work on sustainable economic development in sub-Saharan Africa, before taking each of the areas highlighted in the HCP/World Bank report in turn. In each of these sections, the situation in Morocco is described before a case study is introduced, which has addressed similar issues in a sub-Saharan emerging economy.

I conclude that Morocco's demographic transition (characterised by a rise in population growth followed by a fall in fertility and mortality) must be accompanied by an economic structural transformation; otherwise the demographic dividend cannot be reaped. Supply-side interventions are essential in tackling the three areas mentioned in the HCP/World Bank report, and the case studies from sub-Saharan Africa are proven examples of these, but such efforts only present part of the picture. As I demonstrate through a number of case studies from the work of the Challenges Group, a range of complementary demand-side policies and investments needs to be implemented to improve the macroeconomic environment to assure both sustainable economic growth and social inclusion. The need to capture the energy and potential of Moroccan youth is urgent to prevent them from increasing the ranks of the long-term unemployed or never employed.

Enterprising Solutions to Global Challenges

The case studies presented here are the work of the Challenges Group in sub-Saharan Africa. The Challenges Group is a group of non-profits, social enterprises and impact businesses which devises and implements enterprising solutions to global challenges. Departing from the usual model of grant-aided development assistance, Challenges brings together communities of common interest to grow economies sustainably and in a participatory manner from the bottom up. Challenges intervenes most commonly in three main areas:

1. The provision of accredited, practical business skills training and practice to young people
2. Support for micro, small and medium-sized enterprises to collaborate, develop and grow, often harnessing the skills and energy of women and youth
3. The development of innovative solutions, partnerships and knowledge transfer (south-south and north-south) to overcome barriers to further growth and development

Inclusion

The first area for improvement raised by the HCP/World Bank Report is that of inclusion of women in the workforce. The percentage of Moroccan women working or actively seeking work was 30.6 per cent in 2019 and has barely changed in two decades (World Bank, 2020). According to the ILO (n.d.), 'Only a quarter of young Moroccan women in rural areas are economically active (vs. 56% among men), a rate that drops to just below 12% in urban areas (vs. 32% among men).' Typically, as employees, women in Morocco are over-represented in agriculture and in the light industrial sector but are under-represented in the service and construction sectors (pp. 3–4).

Recognising the need to improve rural income levels and work around the home-making and child-rearing commitments traditionally ascribed to women, the Moroccan government deliberately limited the creation and exploitation of argan oil cooperatives to women under law number 24-83 (Pereira and Santos, 2018, p. 7). While these cooperatives – largely based in the South West Atlantic region around Essaouira and Agadir – have attracted significant interest from foreign aid agencies and have surfed a wave of increased awareness and value of argan oil in international markets, a constant criticism has been the lack of support for women to build capacity to actually run cooperatives (Omari and Elkandoussi, 2013). In practice, this means that men occupy managerial positions and rural women – often poorly educated and unaware of the principles of cooperatives – earn day wages rather than dividends.[3] Furthermore, while international agencies are optimistic about the potential of the argan sector for rural development and female inclusion, the presence of intermediaries and foreign companies in the supply chain raises concerns regarding profits for producers (El Ouadi, 2018). According to local estimates, over 90 per cent of Morocco's argan oil export is in bulk, with limited access for women's cooperatives to international markets and the lion's share of incomes going to middlemen and larger businesses able to guarantee consistency (through more mechanised, less traditional production methods), quality and organic certification (Zhong, n.d.)

In Rwanda, the Coffee Market Building for Peace and Prosperity Project by Challenges works with eight coffee cooperatives and is delivered by the in-country office of Challenges in Kigali (Figure 1.1). Although officially a 'market-building' programme, the approach is holistic, providing a model for cooperative agri-businesses to grow sustainably by improving the human capital of local people, equipping them with business-relevant skills, enabling

3 Based on the author's own research and interviews in Essaouira (2013–14). For further qualitative data and anecdotal evidence, see also various blog posts by companies active in the Moroccan argan and tourism sector: https://www.journeybeyondtravel.com/blog/morocco-coop-shopping-secrets.html; https://saadiaorganics.com/blogs/all/107768007-argan-oil-cooperatives-in-morocco-the-good-the-bad-and-the-unbelievable and https://kahina-givingbeauty.com/the-truth-about-argan-cooperatives/.

Figure 1.1 Woman coffee growers in Rwanda develop their understanding of the business skills needed to operate their farms. The training is developed by Challenges Worldwide using best practice guidance from the Chartered Management Institute, United Kingdom.

the increase of volume and sales, supporting product quality improvements and promoting environmentally friendly agricultural best practices leading to Fairtrade and/or organic certification.

Challenges is one of only 14 strategic partners of the Chartered Management Institute (CMI), United Kingdom. CMI content is adapted to accommodate literacy levels, local languages and gender dimensions in the provision of tailored training in business management capacity. Support is also provided on access to capital for individuals and businesses, on clean and constant power and water and on rural-urban market linkages.

In addition to the training of cooperative farmers and management, Challenges has provided management and leadership training, translated into Kinyarwanda and delivered by local trainers to over one hundred young Rwandans. In parallel, Challenges worked with local organisations to develop a term loan product and a working capital credit line (accessed via MTN Mobile Money, a mobile phone–based service enabling users to store funds, send/receive money and make payments and other transactions), which are currently being piloted with three youth-led off-farm rural businesses. The remaining business plans continue to receive technical support.

By the end of year three (March 2020) of the five-year programme, 40–50 per cent of an estimated eight hundred training recipients of the Rwandan Coffee Project working in cooperatives will have been women. The training these women are receiving has helped increase their engagement in running of cooperatives, supported improved co-op governance and delivered better representation at higher levels in the structure of the cooperatives. While the overall percentage of female training representation has increased year-on-year, it is important to point out that coffee cooperative workers in Rwanda are predominantly male. The specific targeting of women by this programme has enabled them to engage in a space with more agency and accountability than was previously possible.

By combining training and interventions designed to break down structural barriers to business development and growth, the Challenges model has the potential to affect real change. The Challenges approach in Rwanda has been so successful that opportunities are being explored to transfer the model to Malawi and Uganda (Figure 1.2).

Figure 1.2 Business development officers in Malawi learn the essential business, training and facilitation skills to deliver the CROPS (Creating Robust Opportunities for Crop Production and Sale) programme, a Scottish government funded project to utilise value addition centres (VACs) throughout the country, launched by Challenges. Liza, a senior training coordinator with Challenges, travelled from Rwanda, where she trains female-led cooperatives, to deliver the training in Malawi.

Whether the approach taken is a gender exclusive one (such as Morocco's argan cooperative policy) or a gender inclusive one (like the Rwanda Coffee Project), the key is to make it genuinely holistic to secure effective outcomes for whole communities. Without strategic capacity building, supply chain support and access to capital investment, Morocco's argan cooperative policy has delivered limited tangible socio-economic benefits. A Challenges-style approach, combining these aspects, would be an effective addition to a pure policy measure.

Job creation

In the past 15 years, GDP growth in Morocco has averaged 3.2 per cent – around half the level estimated to be necessary to create jobs for the 300,000 working-age people entering the labour market annually (HCP and World Bank, 2017b). According to official statistics, only 7,000 jobs were created in the second quarter of 2019 compared to 117,000 jobs in the same quarter in 2018 (Kasraoui, 2019). This suggests a strong requirement for demand-side ALMPs, but these alone will not be enough.

Small and medium-sized enterprises (SMEs) are widely considered to be the drivers of economic growth, especially in emerging economies. They represent about 90 per cent of businesses and more than 50 per cent of employment worldwide, making them significant players in job creation and economic development (World Bank, n.d., 'SMEs'). In the Moroccan context, SMEs and micro-businesses face numerous constraints which hinder growth and job creation opportunities, including corruption, a mismatch of skills in the workforce, weak competitiveness, competition from the informal sector, high levels of bureaucracy and comparatively high labour costs (particularly employer on costs) for those staff who are fully declared (HCP and World Bank, 2017a, p. 8).

The potential impact of vocational training and employability programmes in job creation (as well as skills improvement) is recognised but inadequately realised in Morocco. A network of profession and skills hubs was announced in April 2019 building on the existing network of National Office for Vocational Training and Promotion (OFPPT) vocational colleges (USAID, 2016; Lindsey, 2017). A key issue, however, is that vocational training is seen as an alternative to, rather than as a supplement to, university-level education. In a speech delivered in August 2019 in Al Hoceima, the epicentre of the previous years' *Hirak Rif*[4] protests, King Mohammed VI emphasised the need for a shift in expectations:

4 *Hirak Rif* was a mass protest movement based in the northern Rif area of Morocco, active between October 2016 and June 2017. The protesters' demands included

> I wish to insist, once again, on the importance of vocational training, especially in villages and suburban areas, to provide youths with skills, and thereby enable them to enter the labour market and contribute to the country's development. Passing the baccalaureate exam and going to university is not a privilege; it is just a phase in the education process.

From 2015 to 2018, the Challenges Group operated a multi-year, multi-country youth volunteering programme called the International Citizen Service (ICS) in partnership with the United Kingdom's Department for International Development (DfID) and Voluntary Service Overseas (VSO). Young Africans were trained in business skills and then placed in social enterprises to perform intensive analysis of SME performance and implement improvements. The programme worked with 650 businesses across Uganda, Zambia, Rwanda and Ghana. Over 70 per cent of these enterprises reported an increase in their workforce following the intervention. In some cases, they employed the young person who had undertaken the placement; in others the business diagnostics and improvements process made efficiency savings which enabled the enterprise to take on more staff. There was a 51 per cent net total workforce increase. Over 60 per cent of participant enterprises reported an increase in revenue following the placement.

On the part of the youth participants, following their training and placement, 90 per cent of volunteers self-reported strongly positive or positive skills developments across 9 out of 10 key skill development areas. Full and part-time employment increased among the participants; 86 per cent of these roles were graduate- to manager-level positions and only 6 per cent were internships. While some of the uptake of employment could be accounted for by a natural progression from study to employment, the data demonstrated that post-placement transition to employment was high among programme participants. This is supported by 77 per cent of those in employment crediting the placement and training with their ability to secure employment.

One area where Morocco has received significant foreign direct investment (FDI) and which has now surpassed remittances as the key source of foreign currency income is tourism (Morikawa, 2015, p. 27). Underlining the potential of this sector, the Moroccan government's Vision 2020 tourism strategy

recognition of language and cultural rights of Riffians, release of political prisoners, human rights, social justice and local infrastructure investment in this area seen as long marginalised by ruling elites.

aims to double the number of jobs in the sector over 2012 to almost 1 million jobs by 2020 (Roudies, 2013).[5]

The focus of the Moroccan government on attracting FDI as an engine of growth is an example of the importance of macroeconomic measures in addition to specific ALMPs. However, while governments may be attracted to high-profile megaprojects financed by foreign partners (Bogaert, 2018), the importance of SMEs – either local or foreign-owned – in job creation must not be overlooked. The World Bank (n.d., 'SMEs') estimates 70 per cent of jobs in emerging markets are created by SMEs, including most formal jobs, making them a key target for job creation interventions – both in quantity and quality. For SMEs to play their role, they need to have internal capacity and an external business environment which is conducive to growth. Externalities include 'access to strategic resources, such as skills, knowledge networks, and finance, as well as public investments in areas such as education and training, innovation and infrastructure' (OECD, 2017, p. 5). The Challenges approach, which utilises the skills and energy of trained young people to boost internal capacity and manage externalities, is a useful model in this regard.

Given the high levels of informality in every sector in Morocco, covered in greater detail in the next section, it is important to ensure that stable jobs are created with a living wage, contracts and social security. One way the ICS programme has done this is to ensure that young people moving into employment are able to describe the value they can add to an enterprise and that they deliver this value through the relevance of their skills.

Job quality

Youth in Morocco tend to be engaged in informal, precarious employment with neither contracts nor social security (Morikawa, 2015, p. 12). Those with lower education levels are most likely to be employed in the informal economy (HCP and World Bank, 2017b, p. 17), that is, without recourse to legal workers' rights and/or in unincorporated entities. Data suggests that more formal enterprises employ higher skilled workers, who are better paid and more productive (p. 9).

HCP and World Bank estimate that 59 per cent of jobs in Morocco are in the informal economy (p. 9). Others put the share of informal employment in labour force as high as almost 80 per cent in Morocco, far higher than its North Africa neighbours (Dufrénot, 2018). The worst affected non-agricultural

5 This goal is likely to be in jeopardy, given the global travel limitations resulting from the 2020 COVID-19 pandemic. At the time of writing, the Moroccan government had not yet recalibrated this strategy.

sector is the commercial sector, which features a high number of micro and family businesses (HCP, 2016, p. 5).

A study commissioned by the General Confederation of Enterprises of Morocco (CGEM) in 2014 found 20 per cent of legal non-agricultural activities were conducted on an informal basis, representing potentially almost MAD 170 billion (€16 bn) in untaxed revenues (Elouazi, 2018). Agriculture, which in 2018 represented 38 per cent of jobs but only 12 per cent of GDP, is measured separately (World Bank 2018c; 2019c). The proportion of employment without contracts is overwhelmingly high for rural areas (almost 100 per cent for women and 94 per cent for men), as well as for urban men (86 per cent) (Morikawa, 2015, p. 12). Of all agricultural employment, estimates suggest around 40 per cent of jobs are completely unpaid, supplementing a significant proportion of precarious (seasonal, impacted by climate change and/or poorly remunerated), but nonetheless paid, positions (Dadush, 2017).

Underemployment is also an issue in Morocco, with the most educated being the least employed and those unable or unwilling to wait for a job commensurate with their skills taking something for which they are overqualified in order to earn something and progress in their lives (ILO, 2017, p. 6; Boudarbat and Ajbilou, 2007, p. 21). The IMF (2019, p. 6) estimates underemployment at around 10 per cent (16 per cent for youth).

The strategic objective of the Youth to Work programme by Challenges in Uganda is to position and equip young people with skills and opportunities to create economic and employment changes across the economy for sustainable and measurable impact. It is the flagship employability programme within Futuremakers by Standard Chartered, the bank's global initiative to tackle inequality and promote greater economic inclusion for young people in local communities, which is undertaken as part of its global social responsibility effort. In parallel to CMI-accredited business skills training, 40 young people are undertaking a practical placement in one of 40 small and growing businesses. Furthermore, up to 200 staff in those businesses will receive business skills training and, through a train-the-trainer approach, the 40 young people will also impart key business skills to around 400 university students. The demand for such initiatives among Ugandan youth is validated by the 800 applications received for 40 places.

Having young people strategically placed in businesses helps leverage business skills improvements, efficiency and investment readiness, which in turn will unlock opportunities for growth, formalisation and job creation up and down the supply chain. The young people are supported in a placement which caters to both their own skills and development requirements as well as those of the SMEs. This approach helps improve job quality by offering opportunities to young people to prove their value to small businesses both by demonstrating the relevance of their skills to the business and by identifying efficiency savings and growth opportunities which might help fund a new position.

The Challenges model currently being implemented in Uganda and already proven elsewhere demonstrates the necessity for a holistic approach which addresses both skills and employability through technical and vocational education and training (TVET) in parallel with developing opportunities for job creation through the business diagnostics and business improvement work conducted during the placements. By improving skills in young people and the capacity of SMEs to grow, both become agents of change in developing a micro- and macroeconomic business environment aimed at growth.

Conclusion

The demographic dividend is not a given. Morocco's youth face severe economic and social exclusion hampering not only their ability to earn a living, but also their transition to adulthood, of which marriage is a key cultural marker (Arnett, 2012, p. 48). Demographic transition must be accompanied by an economic structural transformation to promote not only growth but also social cohesion and reconciliation in the face of a new wave of protest across the region (Daragahi, 2019).

Moroccan youth need opportunities not only to improve their skills, but also to apply them in quality jobs. In the context of a neoliberal globalised economy where the state is shrinking, secure public sector employment is declining and the private sector is seen as the motor of economic growth. The SME strata of the economy is essential in this effort.

ALMPs need to combine supply-side and demand-side measures. Supply-side interventions such as the TVET and entrepreneurship programmes proposed by Challenges, which are proven to improve skills, job opportunities and job quality while supporting the growth of individual SMEs and supply chains, are a potentially useful model for economies such as Morocco, but they cannot be effective in isolation. They must be accompanied by demand-side interventions such as regulatory measures aimed at influencing employers' decisions regarding recruitment, termination, advancement and inclusion (Frøyland et al., 2019).

The scale of Morocco's youth bulge and the closing window of opportunity over the next five years heighten the risks, but also the potential rewards. A reduction in unemployment has the potential to 'unleash resources to invest in education, infrastructure, health, and other productive areas' (Bloom et al., 2017, p. 72), but only if a holistic approach is applied.

The interventions applied and proven by Challenges in sub-Saharan Africa could be translated to the Moroccan context, but as Frøyland et al. (2019) argue, it is not only the jobless who must be 'activated', but also employers.

References

Arnett, J. J. 2012. *Adolescent Psychology around the World*. New York: Psychology.

Bloom, D., Kuhn, M., and Prettner, K. 2017. 'Africa's Prospects for Enjoying a Demographic Dividend'. *Journal of Demographic Economics* 83, no. 1, 63–76.

Bogaert, K. 2018. *Globalized Authoritarianism: Megaprojects, Slums, and Class Relations in Urban Morocco*. Minneapolis: University of Minnesota Press.

Boudarbat, B., and Ajbilou, A. 2007. 'Youth Exclusion in Morocco: Context, Consequences, and Policies'. Middle East Youth Initiative Working Paper no. 5, September (online). Available at: https://www.meyi.org/uploads/3/2/0/1/32012989/boudarbat_and_ajbilou_-_youth_exclusion_in_morocco-context_consequences_and_policies.pdf (accessed 4 December 2019).

Chraibi, Y. 2019. *Les diplômés sont les plus touchés par le chômage, selon le HCP*, H24info (online) (last updated 27 February 2019). Available at: https://www.h24info.ma/maroc/maroc-les-diplomes-sont-les-plus-touches-par-le-chomage/ (accessed 13 December 2019).

Dadush, U. 2017. 'Moroccan Job Market Issues, and Labour Trends in the Middle East and North Africa' (online) (last updated 7 December 2017). Available at: https://bruegel.org/2017/12/moroccan-job-market-issues-and-labour-trends-in-the-middle-east-and-north-africa/ (accessed 14 December 2019).

Daragahi, B. 2019. 'Why the Middle East Is Being Rocked by New Wave of Protests'. *Independent* (online) (last updated 1 November 2019). Available at: https://www.independent.co.uk/news/world/middle-east/middle-east-protests-lebanon-iraq-algeria-arab-spring-sudan-a9181411.html (accessed 14 December 2019).

Dufrénot, G. 2018. 'The Third Demographic Dividend: Measuring the "Demographic Tax" in the Arab Countries in Transition'. CEPII Working Paper no. 2018-15 – September (online). Available at: http://www.cepii.fr/PDF_PUB/wp/2018/wp2018-15.pdf (accessed 13 December 2019).

El Ouadi, I. 2018. 'Argan Oil: Is Outside Exploitation of Morocco's Liquid Gold Imperiling Local Coops?' *Inside Arabia* (online) (last updated 25 November 2018). Available at: https://insidearabia.com/argan-oil-outside-exploitation-imperiling-local-coops/ (accessed 19 June 2020).

Elouazi, S. 2018. 'Informal Economy Represents More than 20% of Morocco's GDP: Study'. *Morocco World News* (online) (last updated 7 April 2018). Available at: https://www.moroccoworldnews.com/2018/04/243990/informal-economy-morocco-gdp-study/ (accessed 14 December 2019).

Frøyland, K., Andreassen, T. A., and Innvær, S. 2019. 'Contrasting Supply-Side, Demand-Side and Combined Approaches to Labour Market Integration'. *Journal of Social Policy* 48, no. 2 (April), 311–28.

Harkat, T., and Driouchi, A. 2017. 'Demographic Dividend Economic Development in Arab Countries'. MPRA Paper (online) (last updated 22 November 2017). Available at: https://mpra.ub.uni-muenchen.de/82880/ (accessed 13 December 2019).

Haut Commissariat au Plan (HCP). 2016. 'Présentation des résultats de l'Enquête Nationale sur le Secteur Informel 2013/2014' (online) (last updated 12 October 2016). Available at: https://www.hcp.ma/file/183897/ (accessed 14 December 2019).

Haut Commissariat au Plan (HCP) and World Bank. 2017a. 'Le marché du travail au Maroc : défis et opportunités' (online) (last updated November 2017). Available at: https://www.worldbank.org/en/country/morocco/publication/labor-market-in-morocco-challenges-and-opportunities (accessed 13 December 2019).

———. 2017b. 'Labour Market in Morocco: Challenges and Opportunities' (online) (last updated November 2017). Available at: http://documents.worldbank.org/curated/en/529381523251399925/pdf/125041-WP-FRENCH-PUBLIC-Le-march%C3%A9-du-travail-au-Maroc-23-Nov.pdf (accessed 13 December 2019).

Ighobor, K. 2017. 'Africa's Jobless Youth Cast a Shadow Over Economic Growth'. Africa Renewal, Special Edition on Youth 2017 (online). Available at: https://www.un.org/africarenewal/magazine/special-edition-youth-2017/africas-jobless-youth-cast-shadow-over-economic-growth (accessed 13 December 2019).

International Labour Organisation (ILO). 2017. 'Youth and Employment in North Africa: A Regional Overview' (online) (last updated September 2017). Available at: https://www.ilo.org/wcmsp5/groups/public/---africa/---ro-addis_ababa/documents/meetingdocument/wcms_577306.pdf (accessed 13 December 2019).

———. N.d. 'Morocco – Young Women's Employment and Empowerment in the Rural Economy' (online). Available at: https://www.ilo.org/wcmsp5/groups/public/---ed_emp/documents/publication/wcms_622767.pdf (accessed 13 December 2019).

International Monetary Fund (IMF). 2016. 'Country Report No. 16/36, "Morocco"' (online) (last updated February 2016). Available at: https://www.imf.org/external/pubs/ft/scr/2016/cr1636.pdf (accessed 13 December 2019).

———. 2019. 'Country Report No. 19/231, "Morocco"' (online) (last updated July 2019). Available at: https://www.imf.org/~/media/Files/Publications/CR/2019/1MAREA2019004.ashx (accessed 14 December 2019).

Kasraoui, S. 2019. 'Morocco Records Significant Decrease in Job Creation in 2nd Quarter of 2019'. Morocco World News (online). Available at: https://www.moroccoworldnews.com/2019/08/279918/morocco-significant-decrease-job-creation/ (accessed 13 December 2019).

King Mohammed VI. 2019. 'Discours à la Nation à l'occasion du 66-ème anniversaire de la Révolution du Roi et du Peuple'. Agence Marocaine de Presse (online) (last updated 20 August 2019). Available at: http://www.mapnews.ma/fr/activites-royales/sa-majest%C3%A9-le-roi-adresse-un-discours-%C3%A0-la-nation-%C3%A0-loccasion-du-66-%C3%A8me (accessed 14 December 2019).

Lindsey, U. 2017. 'In Morocco, a Big Push for Vocational Education'. Al-Fanar Media (online) (last updated 23 May 2017). Available at: https://www.al-fanarmedia.org/2017/05/morocco-big-push-vocational-education/ (accessed 14 December 2019).

Mason, A., Lee, R., Abrigo, M., and Lee, S.-H. 2017. 'Support Ratios and Demographic Dividends: Estimates for the World'. United Nations Department of Economic and Social Affairs Technical Paper 2017/1 (online). Available at: https://www.un.org/en/development/desa/population/publications/pdf/technical/TP2017-1.pdf (accessed 13 December 2019).

Morikawa, Y. 2015. 'The Opportunities and Challenges for Female Labor Force Participation in Morocco'. Brookings Global Economy and Development Working

Paper no. 86, July 2015. Available at: https://www.brookings.edu/wp-content/uploads/2016/07/female-labor-force-participation.pdf (accessed 14 December 2019).

Omari, S., and Elkandoussi, F. 2013. 'The Marketing of Women's Argan Cooperatives: Challenges and Opportunities'. *International Journal of Business and Social Science* 4, no. 6 (June) (online). Available from: https://pdfs.semanticscholar.org/9148/f8a8372f3a69b3fc7806f2560f72b0fc47d8.pdf (accessed 13 December 2019).

Organisation for Economic Co-operation and Development (OECD). 2017. 'Meeting of the OECD Council at Ministerial Level' (online). Available at: https://www.oecd.org/mcm/documents/C-MIN-2017-8-EN.pdf (accessed 14 December 2019).

Pereira, L., and Santos, N. 2018. 'Maroc Investir dans l'action collective: quelles opportunités pour les coopératives du secteur agro-alimentaire?' (online). Available at: http://www.fao.org/3/CA1198FR/ca1198fr.pdf (accessed 13 December 2019).

Rachidi, I. 2019. 'Morocco's Crackdown Won't Silence Dissent'. Foreign Policy (online) (last updated 19 January 2019). Available at: https://foreignpolicy.com/2019/01/16/moroccos-crackdown-wont-silence-dissent-maroc-hirak-amdh/ (accessed 13 December 2019).

Roudies, N. 2013. 'Vision 2020 for Tourism in Morocco'. Delivered to UN Expert Group Meeting on Ecotourism, Poverty Reduction & Environmental Protection on 29 October. Available at: https://sustainabledevelopment.un.org/content/documents/4104roudies.pdf (accessed 14 December 2019).

Sathar, Z. A., Royan, R., and Bongaarts, J. 2013. 'Capturing the Demographic Dividend in Pakistan' (online). Available at: https://www.popcouncil.org/uploads/pdfs/2013_CapturingDemoDivPak.pdf (accessed 13 December 2019).

United Nations Population Fund. 2017. 'Demographic Dividend' (online) (last updated 16 May 2017). Available at: https://arabstates.unfpa.org/en/topics/demographic-dividend-6 (accessed 13 December 2019).

USAID Career Centre. ca. 2016. 'Career Centers en Région'. VCC Career Center (online). Available at: https://vcc.careercenter.ma/vcc/careercenter (accessed 14 December 2019).

World Bank. 2012. 'The Challenges of Youth Inclusion in Morocco' (online) (last updated 14 May 2012). Available at: https://www.worldbank.org/en/news/feature/2012/05/14/challenge-of-youth-inclusion-in-morocco (Accessed 13 December 2019).

———. 2015. 'Social Protection and Labour Brief Morocco' (online) (last updated 26 May 2015). Available at: http://documents.worldbank.org/curated/en/485991468190443363/pdf/103119-WP-P133498-Box394855B-PUBLIC-A2I-REQUEST-SPL-Morocco-Draft-Policy-Note-v12.pdf (accessed 13 December 2019).

———. ca. 2018a 'GDP Growth (Annual %) – Morocco' (online). Available at: https://data.worldbank.org/indicator/NY.GDP.MKTP.KD.ZG?locations=MA (accessed 13 December 2019).

———. ca. 2018b. 'GDP Per Capita (Current US$) – Sub-Saharan Africa' (online). Available at: https://data.worldbank.org/indicator/NY.GDP.PCAP.CD?locations=ZG&most_recent_value_desc=true (accessed 13 December 2019).

———. ca. 2018c. 'Agriculture, Forestry, and Fishing, Value Added (% of GDP)' (online). Available at: https://data.worldbank.org/indicator/NV.AGR.TOTL.ZS (accessed 14 December 2019).

———. ca. 2019a. 'Age Dependency Ratio (% of Working-Age Population) – Morocco' (online). Available at: https://data.worldbank.org/indicator/SP.POP.DPND?locations=MA (accessed 13 December 2019).

———. 2019b. 'Doing Business 2020' (online). Available at: https://openknowledge.worldbank.org/bitstream/handle/10986/32436/9781464814402.pdf (p. 4) (accessed 13 December 2019).

———. 2019c. 'Gender Data Portal' (online). Available at: http://datatopics.worldbank.org/gender/country/morocco (accessed 19 June 2020).

———. 2020. 'Employment in Agriculture (% of Total Employment) (Modeled ILO Estimate)' (online). Available at: https://data.worldbank.org/indicator/SL.AGR.EMPL.ZS?locations=MA (accessed 14 December 2019).

World Bank. N.d. 'Fact Sheet' (online). Available at: https://www.worldbank.org/en/webarchives/archive?url=httpzzxxweb.worldbank.org/archive/website01418/WEB/0__C-301.HTM (accessed 13 December 2019).

World Bank. N.d. 'Small and Medium Enterprises (SMEs) Finance' (online). Available at: https://www.worldbank.org/en/topic/smefinance (accessed 13 December 2019).

Youssef, H., Elden, N. M. K., and Ali, H. A. 2018. 'Realising the Prospects of the Demographic Dividend in Selected Arab Countries'. *Epidemiology Biostatics and Public Health* 15, no. 3. Available at: https://ebph.it/article/view/12888 (accessed 13 December 2019).

Zhong, X. n.d. 'Value-Added Argan Oil Increasing Women's Independence in Rural Morocco' (online). Available at: https://www.unido.org/news/value-added-argan-oil-increasing-womens-independence-rural-morocco (accessed 13 December 2019).

Chapter 2

SOCIAL MEDIA AS A WEAPON: HOW THE YOUTH IN RIO DE JANEIRO'S FAVELAS FIGHT POLICE VIOLENCE

Julia Jaroschewski

On the evening of 2 April 2015, Betinho Casas Novas gets pictures and news on his smartphone of a boy who was killed, grabs his gear and runs. As fast as he can, he runs through the alleys of the Complexo do Alemão, a favela consisting of 25 settlements whose thousands of tiny brick houses stretch across several valleys and mountains north of Rio de Janeiro, Brazil. Suddenly, shots roar through the alleys.

Forty minutes pass: shootings between police and drug gangs stall his progress. By telephone, relatives of the dead boy guide him to the crime scene. When he arrives, the people applaud him – because he is one of them, a guy from the favela. But Casas Novas is afraid that he will pass out. 'Filming a dead boy with a hole in his head, bleeding, his body destroyed – I didn't know if I could do it', he says.

That night, he just begins to film, takes photos and lets himself be told what has happened. Terezinha de Jesus Ferreira was sitting in front of the television with her son Eduardo. The 10-year-old went to the door to wait for his sister. All of a sudden, there was a crash. Terezinha ran outside and found her son dead in a pool of blood. Struck by a single shot to the back of his head, from a distance of 10 meters, by a policeman.

Casas Novas documents the tumult: how neighbours gather at the scene, how policemen push the crowd away from the body at gunpoint, how the mother almost collapses. Children cry. Fear of the police mixes with anger and powerlessness. 'Murderers!' women scream. 'Cowards!' He publishes the photos on social media – Facebook, WhatsApp and Twitter. They are immediately clicked on and shared.

The video, which he edited during the night, was watched by thousands on YouTube within a short time span; today it stands at 16,000 clicks. TV stations request Casas Novas for the footage for their coverage. 'The big media didn't come to the favela that night', he says. 'Luckily, my video was so successful – otherwise Eduardo would have been just another number in the statistics.'

Youth Falling Victim to the Violence

In the violence-ridden favelas of Complexo do Alemão, the police often act as if they are above the law. For decades, the favelas – Brazil's informal settlements, constructed organically by the poor and migrants – were like forgotten places; not registered on official maps, neglected by the government, governed by drug gangs. A quarter of the inhabitants of Rio de Janeiro – about 1.4 million people – live in these settlements. More than a thousand favelas crowd the hills in the middle of rich districts and extend the edges of Rio (IBGE, 2011).

Brazil's age structure has been very favourable since the 1990s, but the country has struggled to capitalise on its demographic dividend. According to the Berlin Institute for Population and Development (2015, p. 1), Brazil has seen an economic upturn and a certain decrease in poverty and inequality in the past decades. But significant parts of the population still face severe economic and social challenges – and Brazil's favelas and their inhabitants pay the prize for failed urban politics and misguided public investments, suffering from a lack of access to basic infrastructure, health services and security (Soares, 2019, p. 141f.).

The potential of the youth in the favelas is hampered by everyday violence. Gangs, police and militia fight for control of the impoverished settlements. Gunfights are a psychological burden on children, make access to school more difficult, lead to high rates of cancelled lessons and impact the children's scholastic achievements (Monteiro and Rocha, 2017, p. 4). A lower education level, but also discrimination, makes it difficult for youth from the favelas to gain access to the formal labour market.

Thousands of children and young people have become victims of the drug war – especially young black boys and men (Cerqueira et al., 2018; Soares, 2019, p. 24). According to the Brazilian Public Security Forum, the country registered more than 61,000 violent deaths in 2016, a growth of 3.8 per cent compared to 2015. Violent deaths caused by police officers increased by 25.8 per cent. Between 2009 and 2013, more than 11,000 people were killed in police operations – most of them in favelas (Fórum Brasileiro de Segurança Pública, 2016).

The Voice of the Favelas

In earlier times, what happened in a favela remained in the favela. The dead were invisible. A boy shot to death? One of many, not worth the news. In the case of Eduardo – the 10-year-old killed in the Complexo do Alemão – the police later claim that the boy was hit by a ricochet when policemen and members of a drug gang fired at each other. 'The only shot I heard was the one that killed my son', the boy's mother says. Maybe one of the policemen pulled the trigger too fast, maybe he thought the boy was a member of the drug gang.

The projectile that killed Eduardo has disappeared. Residents claim to have seen police collecting bullets at the scene. It is also to the credit of Betinho Casas Novas and the citizen media platform Voz da Comunidade (The voice of the favela), for which he works, that the authorities have started to investigate this case – and the blood-drenched body of a boy in blue shorts has become a symbol of violence in the favelas.

Voz da Comunidade is the most prominent example of a shift in power between the state and its inhabitants in the Brazilian favelas. Through their direct and unmasked reporting, young Brazilian citizen journalists like Casas Novas give their homeland, the poor areas of the metropolis, a powerful voice on the internet – so loud that it can no longer be ignored.

The inhabitants make public the violence that does not officially exist. On Twitter, Facebook, Instagram and their own blogs and websites, they provide their perspectives, present their everyday lives and denounce grievances (Jaroschewski, 2015; Muggah, 2015). 'Through the internet, the favela has a voice, everyone has a mobile phone with which they can express their opinions and produce their own news', says Betinho Casas Novas. The poor, who haven't had a lobby for a long time, thus create a counter-public pressure on TV stations and major newspapers, which like to rely on official press releases in their reports, as well as on the police and politicians. The voice of a single desperate mother on the street can be subdued. But no one can now afford to ignore the voice of the favela on the internet (Nafi, 2019).

Betinho Casas Novas sits in the editorial office of Voz da Comunidade in Morro do Adeus, one of the settlements of the Complexo do Alemão. It is almost morning of the next day as he edits a video on a 13-inch laptop. Next to him, Rene Silva checks his messages on an iPhone. Silva is editor-in-chief of the favela portal.

The editorial office is sparsely furnished: there is a sofa and four computers. Here, they edit material for the website they run and distribute information they receive from residents via WhatsApp, Facebook and Twitter. And they work against the criminalisation of innocent citizens. After Eduardo's death,

Figure 2.1 Betinho Casas Novas. Smartphones as witnesses of violence: The photographer Betinho Casas Novas documents what happens in the favelas of Rio de Janeiro, for example, shootings and police violence. Credit: Julia Jaroschewski.

photos of a boy with an assault rifle in his hand circulated online. They were supposed to be pictures of Eduardo. The reporters checked the pictures and proved that they showed a young member of a drug gang, not Eduardo. On such days, they rarely leave their offices, consumed by the tasks at hand.

Casas Novas and Silva both grew up here (Figure 2.1). Fragile houses, stacked on top of each other, floor by floor. Stinking alleys, where the sewage runs, small shops, football bars close together, dogs barking, children on the street. Everyone knows everyone here; there is no privacy. The cousin lives across the street, the parents on the floor below – the favela is always family, but also headquarters of Comando Vermelho, one of Brazil's biggest crime syndicates.

The initials of the gang can be found on the walls of the brick houses: 'CV', in black or red capital letters, with graffiti. The walls of the houses are scarred by bullets from the gunfire between the drug gangs and the police. Journalists from major news outlets often venture into this area with bulletproof vests and police protection. Here the drug gang is law. The gang replaces the state, collects taxes, controls public transport, organises parties, take care of garbage collection and provides security within the favela (Amorim, 2010, p. 118). The two young men also grew up with the drug soldiers, young men who walk through the favela with assault rifles, often no older than themselves.

Favela Influencer with a Hundred Thousand Followers

For a long time, the favelas of the beach metropolis have been regarded as disgraceful spots in the city, a breeding ground for young gangsters. At the age of 11, Rene Silva wants to show that there is also another life here, one which the wealthy in the suburbs know nothing of and want nothing to do with. He founded the newspaper *Voz da Comunidade*, initially as part of a school project. The *Voz* describes everyday life, the other face of the favela. The first editions are hardly more than two double sheets, laid out on a school computer, copied and folded. It starts circulation with a mere one hundred copies (Abreu and Silva, 2013, p. 27).

The monthly newspaper finds its audience because it bridges a gap. 'The people here distrust the mass media because they only write about shootings and violence and don't listen to what the inhabitants of the favelas say', Silva explains. His grandmother's living room becomes an editorial office, and his grandfather buys him his first laptop through 24 monthly instalments. Soon *Voz* is financed by advertisements from local shops. Silva can pay back his grandfather's loan and the circulation rises to three thousand. Then Rene Silva discovers Twitter – and Twitter discovers him.

On 28 November 2010, three thousand soldiers stormed the settlements to occupy the Complexo do Alemão (see Figure 2.2) before the World Cup and Olympic Games – police presence is supposed to pacify a total of around two hundred favelas in Rio, disarming the drug gangs. Rene Silva, then 17, and his reporters tweet from the favela: 'Violent shootings in the Complexo do Alemão now, people.' And: 'The drug dealers threw a grenade at policemen!!!' They film helicopters roaring over the favela. They are the only ones who report live – the whole of Brazil is watching and Rene Silva himself becomes the voice of the favela, the face of a digital generation living in the slums (Abreu and Silva, 2013, p. 20).

He gives interviews, gets invited to talk shows. The Brazilian mobile phone provider TIM features him in their advertisements, as does Coca-Cola which flew him to London, where he carried the Olympic torch in 2012. Foundations invite him to New York and India to collaborate and discuss with other committed young activists. He uses sponsorship money from companies, the media and foundations to finance the editorial offices, and a bank equips the team with iPhones. In 2015, Forbes magazine named him one of the most important Brazilian change makers under the age of 30. Today, Silva has more than 218,000 followers on Twitter and 91,000 on Instagram. WhatsApp

Figure 2.2 Complexo do Alemão. In the favelas of Complexo do Alemão in the north of Rio de Janeiro, drug gangs and police fight each other – and residents are repeatedly caught in the crossfire. Credit: Julia Jaroschewski.

is also a central communication channel for him. New followers and friends from all over the world are added every day.

An Escape – and New Perspectives

About 20 freelance reporters are now on the road for Voz. They not only work as journalists, but also organise events such as concerts. Many young people come by when they have nothing to do – because Voz is a place where they can meet their friends, an escape from the cramped brick houses where they live with their families. Sometimes the office resembles a youth club. Boys and girls sit on the sofa, hang out on the stairs; the television is running in the background.

When the four laptops are occupied, the mobile phone remains. Wi-Fi is available free of charge from the editorial office. Almost everyone taps around on their smartphones and comments on their friends' posts on Facebook or Instagram. 'Tiaagooooo, can you tell me which filter to use?' The world of young people here doesn't seem far away from that of Berlin or Paris.

According to the market research institute Data Popular, almost 80 per cent of young people aged 16–29 in Rio's favelas already had access to the internet as early as 2013, many of them via their mobile phones (UOL, 2013). Even in the favelas of Salvador or Recife in northeastern Brazil or the favelas of São Paulo, more and more residents are using cell phones and apps, setting up online citizen media. Many initiatives are inspired by Rene Silva and the Voz da Comunidade.

Citizens in the Crossfire

The story of the platform reads like a modern-day fairy tale. A school newspaper develops into a media brand that attracts attention in the highest circles of the government and portrays life in the favela as it is, with all its bright and dark sides. But even the makers of Voz watched helplessly as the situation deteriorated dramatically in recent years. Now, after the World Cup 2014 and the Olympic Games 2016, the Complexo do Alemão is more dangerous than ever. The city has classified the Alemão as a 'dangerous area', a risk area. The drug gang is reclaiming its territory.

With the new government of the right-wing conservative president Jair Bolsonaro elected in 2018, the country is more divided than ever. There were plans for the security policy to be strengthened, the military upgraded and criminals punished more severely. Wilson Witzel, the governor of Rio, himself a supporter of the Brazilian right, was counting on a tough security concept for Rio (Machado and Franco, 2019). Emergency forces were to put potential criminals out of action without having to fear punishment (Schweimler, 2019; Muñoz Acebes, 2020). This increased the fear, especially among the young population in the favelas, since racial profiling and prejudice against young black favela inhabitants as suspected integrants of drug gangs led not only to increased controls and arrests, but also to repeated violent assaults by the police (Soares, 2019, pp. 15–16, 43).

With a heavy uniform and a finger on the trigger of the machine gun, the police sneak through the alleys. They entrench themselves in schools and shoot from rooftops into poorly visible paths in battles with drug gangs. For the residents, going to work or school is a life-threatening risk. Silva sometimes has to cancel editorial meetings if he doesn't want to risk one of his reporters being shot. Police against gangs, gangs against police, gangs against gangs – the residents in the crossfire. 'Violence is changing the everyday lives of all residents – today the favela lives in fear', says Betinho Casas Novas.

As soon as another shooting starts, the reporters of Voz warn the people through social networks although they would much rather write about positive things. 'We report so that no one is surprised by a bullet and becomes part of the statistics', says Casas Novas. 'There's no end to the war, and the residents are looking for solutions on the social networks.'

The Brazilians who do not live in favelas also live vicariously through the videos of the favela residents: soldiers jump into a small shop because they are shot at, they shoot back with their machine guns – filmed from the shop, by witnesses of the scene. A motorbike taxi driver is shot from a distance by police officers – captured by a mobile phone camera. The pictures are not glossy: they wobble, they stand on edge, voices roll over. They contradict the rules of any reporting, but they constitute authentic evidence.

This video material reveals the excessive police violence, says Robert Muggah, research director of the Igarapé Institute in Rio de Janeiro, which specialises in public security. 'The elite is now confronted with these rituals of violence and intimidation, and they do not like what they see.' The digital eyewitness accounts contribute to the fact that police officers are being investigated more frequently today – sometimes they even lead to arrests. 'Video footage is now being used in court as evidence, but it is still in the early stages', Muggah explained (Jaroschewski, 2015; Muggah, 2015).

Human rights organisations such as Amnesty International have in recent years increasingly focused on the empowerment of youth and local activists. They specifically train young people in the favelas to use mobile phones and social media for themselves and to report and document police violence and abuse of power and authority (Jaroschewski, 2015; Salomon, 2016). It is precisely because the public and the international community have lost sight of Brazil's problems, the populist president is attracting attention and the access to the everyday hotspots of socio-economic inequality and violence is being reduced that the virtual, mobile work of journalists and activists from the favelas is important (Nafi, 2019.).

Eduardo's mother Terezinha also uses the internet to fight against forgetting her son. In a YouTube video, she holds a photo of her son in front of her chest for 14 minutes, a single shot. 'My life has turned into hell', she says. Due to the public pressure, the family received compensation for pain and suffering, a silent admission of guilt. But the trial of the policemen who shot Eduardo was discontinued in 2016 – also due to lack of evidence (Coelho, 2016). 'They won that little battle, but they won't win the war', Terezinha is convinced. 'As long as I live, I will fight for justice for my son.'

References

Abreu, Sabrina, and Silva, Rene. 2013. *A voz do Alemão: Como Rene Silva e outros jovens ajudaram a mudar a imagem da comunidade.* São Paulo: nVersos.

Amorim, Carlos. 2010. *Assalto ao poder: O crime organizado*. Rio de Janeiro: Record.

Berlin Institute for Population and Development. 2015. 'How to Foster a Dividend: Latecomer Brazil' (online). Available at: https://www.berlin-institut.org/fileadmin/user_upload/Weltbank/final_brazil.pdf (accessed 12 January 2020).

Cerqueira, Daniel, de Lima, Renato Sergio, Bueno, Samira, Neme, Cristina, Ferreira, Helder, Coelho, Danilo, Alves, Paloma Palmieri, Pinheiro, Marina, Astolfi Roberta, and Marques, David. Interns: Milena Reis and Filipe Merian. 2018. *Atlas da Violência 2018*. Fórum Brasileiro de Segurança Pública/Ipea.

Coelho, Henrique. 2016. 'Processo Contra Pms Acusados De Matar Menino Eduardo, No Alemão, É Arquivado' (online). Available at: https://g1.globo.com/rio-de-janeiro/noticia/processo-contra-pms-acusados-de-matar-menino-eduardo-no-alemao-e-arquivado.ghtml (accessed 10 January 2020).

Fórum Brasileiro de Segurança Pública. 2016. 'Ocorrências letais – tabelas' (online). Available at: http://www.forumseguranca.org.br/estatisticas/tableau-ocorrencias (Accessed 30 December 2020).

IBGE. 2011. 'Censo 2010: Resultados' (online). Available at: https://censo2010.ibge.gov.br/en/noticias-censo?busca=1&id=3&idnoticia=2057&view=noticia (accessed 12 March 2020).

Jaroschewski, Julia. 2015. 'Mit Smartphones gegen die Gewalt in Rios berüchtigster Favela'. *Wired Magazin*, 25 August 25. https://www.gq-magazin.de/auto-technik/articles/ausgabe-0915-mit-smartphone-und-blog-gegen-gewalt-und-mord-rio-de-janeiro.

———. 2016. 'Fackel mit Blutspuren'. *taz*, 5 August. https://taz.de/Polizeigewalt-in-Brasilien/!5324134/.

Machado, Leandro, and Franco, Luiza. 2019. '"Aventura jurídica" e "licença para matar": o que dizem juristas sobre excludente de ilicitude em projeto de Bolsonaro'. BBC News Brasil em São Paulo, 23 November. https://www.bbc.com/portuguese/brasil-50522542.

Monteiro, Joana, and Rocha, Rudi. 2017. 'Drug Battles and School Achievement: Evidence from Rio de Janeiro's Favelas'. *Review of Economics and Statistics*, 99(2), 213–28.

Muggah, Robert. 2015. 'Gangsta's Paradise: How Brazil's Criminals (and Police) Use Social Media'. *Americas Quarterly*, 20 August. https://www.americasquarterly.org/article/gangstas-paradise-how-brazils-criminals-and-police-use-social-media/.

Muñoz Acebes, Cesar. 2020. 'Brazil Suffers Its Own Scourge of Police Brutality'. *Americas Quarterly*, 3 June 3. https://www.americasquarterly.org/article/brazil-suffers-its-own-scourge-of-police-brutality/.

Nafi, Tariq. 2019. 'Document, Mobilise, Amplify: The Media Activists in Rio's Favelas'. *Al Jazeera*, 22 September. https://web.archive.org/web/20200922192035/https://www.aljazeera.com/programmes/listeningpost/2019/09/document-mobilise-amplify-media-activists-rio-favelas-190921074122508.html.

Salomon, Josefina. 2016. 'How Brazil's Favelas Are Using Mobile Phones to Fight Back against Police Brutality'. *International Business Times*, 14 September. https://www.ibtimes.co.uk/how-brazils-favelas-are-using-mobile-phones-fight-back-against-police-brutality-1572885.

Schweimler, Daniel. 2019. 'Police Violence Worsens in Brazil's Poor Neighbourhoods Despite Many Questionable Police Killings, No Rio de Janeiro Police Officer Has Yet Been Convicted or Jailed'. *Al Jazeera*, 23 June. https://www.aljazeera.com/news/2019/06/police-violence-worsens-brazils-poor-neighbourhoods-190623162216848.html.

Soares, Luiz Eduardo. 2019. *Desmilitarizar: Segurança pública e direitos humanos*. São Paulo: Boitempo.

UOL. 2013. 'Metade Dos Moradores De Favelas Do País Tem Internet Em Casa, Diz Pesquisa' (online). Available at: https://www.uol.com.br/tilt/noticias/redacao/2013/10/30/metade-das-favelas-do-pais-tem-acesso-a-internet-diz-pesquisa.htm (accessed 12 March 2020).

Chapter 3

MOBILISING HUMAN CAPITAL TO HARNESS THE DEMOGRAPHIC DIVIDEND: THE ROLE OF THE DIASPORA AS ACTORS OF CHANGE IN THE GAMBIA

Kebba-Omar Jagne

As the challenges confronting states become increasingly complex, the nation-building process must become more inclusive and diverse. The way actors are engaged and the kinds of actors engaged must reflect the realities imposed by these challenges to make the structures created around our collective responses inherently resilient. Addressing unemployment, migration and poverty and facilitating access to basic services are key building blocks of national development. Yet, sometimes, their attainment is hindered by the very power structures intended to frame those processes due to a failure to maximise the use of available resources.

The population bulge across Africa, specifically within the demographic most relevant for the labour force, that is, 15- to 35-year-olds, has pushed governments beyond deliberating over the potential existence of a dividend to be earned from this growth, to assessing how the dividend can be harnessed (African Union, 2017). Responses by governments have varied across countries, ranging from science and technology–linked interventions and policy-making, to increasing investments in skills and capacity-building programmes, most notably through entrepreneurship support (African Union, 2017).

Yet, given the annual shortage of seven million jobs across Africa, the current responses are failing to meet this demand for youth entering the workforce (AfDB, 2016). Harnessing the demographic dividend must go hand in hand with managing the sustainability of the growth within the youth demographic, because the ramifications of their joblessness are trans-generational. Furthermore, it affects coordination on the core building blocks already mentioned as part of the nation-building process. Several factors can potentially explain this politico-economic failure, and this chapter explores the human capital aspect of the debate around the demographic dividend, with a focus on the Gambia and a key actor in its diaspora as a change agent.

Due to their remoteness perhaps, it is easy to omit diaspora groups when considering the human capital base of countries. Often, this is linked to the kind of relationship that diasporas share with their home governments. However, regardless of that assessment, diaspora groups continue to be a major contributor to nation-building across developing countries (Migration Policy, 2018). Investments, family ties and religious and sociocultural ties all contribute to maintaining such relationships, which can also be severed for political and security reasons and vice versa.

Global Networks

The dependence on local actors or bilateral arrangements alone cannot suffice in meeting the complex domestic challenges facing governments and communities in these countries (Ofuho, 2009). Diasporas can have access to diverse resources that might not be accessible or readily available in the home country, which can transform the collective responses to such challenges. Particularly in the intervention areas earlier mentioned as key building blocks of nation-building, diaspora involvement is becoming increasingly inevitable.

These global networks of individuals that share common ties with a home country are becoming increasingly complex in their own ways. This complexity includes internal networks within a host country, and across host countries in a global network where commonalities or patterns can also be derived (Migration Policy, 2018). For example, the diaspora in a certain region might be more politically reactive than in another part of the world where that same country's diaspora might place greater value on religious freedom or ease of doing business in the home country.

The Gambia is a small country of two million people in West Africa, surrounded by Senegal on all sides except on the Atlantic seaboard. The west of the country is bordered by the Atlantic Ocean, which makes it a strategic location despite it being the smallest country in the region. Being an anglophone country surrounded by francophone and lusophone countries located between Western Europe and the Americas places it centrally under the Greenwich Mean Time (GMT) zone. This contributes to why the country is often viewed as a gateway into West and sub-Saharan Africa.

Breaking from British colonial rule in 1965, the current episode of the Gambia's political history features a third republic after 52 years under just two parties. During the first republic, which lasted 30 years, the seeds to make the Gambia a tourism- and agriculture-based economy were sown. Other aspects of the economy, which could have complemented this strategy and boosted growth, were ignored (UN-DESA, 2019). Specifically, strategising around better use of the seaport and river transport could have been, and to a large extent still can be, a game changer.

While livelihoods improved under the second republic, it was also a period characterised by authoritarianism and an iron-fist rule. Abuse of power was rife within the political system, and mismanagement shrunk the economy, which became increasingly dependent on remittances over time. In recent years, the remittances' share of GDP has risen to 20 per cent (IFAD, 2017). Perhaps an unintended consequence, it increased the power and influence of the Gambian diaspora around the world, which played a crucial role in unseating the former president Yahya Jammeh in 2016. During his presidency, the international profile of the Gambia changed significantly: from adoration, to reservation, and later ridicule – as he became increasingly polarising, the country became more and more notorious.

Yet, after the change in regime in 2016, the country earned international goodwill and to some degree regained the respect and admiration it had built. On this occasion, it came especially from sub-Saharan Africa, following the military intervention of the Economic Community of West African States (ECOWAS) after Jammeh refused to accept defeat and relinquish power. Within the current political dispensation however, frustration and to a large part confusion have settled over the opportunity provided by the initial excitement that the administration heralding the third republic was always going to enjoy.

When former president Jammeh came to power in 1994, it was through a military coup d'état, which increased the outflow of Gambians, adding to those already fleeing from failing policies under the first regime. The economy was in a state of stagnation due to inefficiencies in socialist-style institutions. A failed coup in 1981 marked a period during which greater numbers of Gambians began relocating to Great Britain, the country's former colonial power.

Brain Drain

The public and private sectors joined hands in trying to boost the economy by building domestic competencies in tourism, but this only temporarily slowed down the decline. Soon, labourers within that industry began migrating to Scandinavia. Naturally, this impacted the labour force given the critical age range of those migrating, that is, 15- to 35-year-olds, in a country of one million people (Faal and Mitchell, 2008). Arguably, this period marks the first major tide of emigration.

With the arrival of Jammeh, the profile of those emigrating gradually changed. From young working-age males with basic schooling, to more educated Gambians from an older demographic, that is, 40 and above (Abdeslam, 2008). This change broadened the destinations Gambians were travelling to, revealing a deeper interest in sub-Saharan Africa and the United States. With the increase in the number of Gambians leaving the country, the volume of remittances flowing into the Gambia was also rising. Remittances were a by-product of the human capital flight or brain drain – the emigration of highly trained or qualified people from their home country, creating a paradox that would prove to be costly (Ul Haque and Kim, 1994).

Between 1995 and 2010, the Gambia often ranked among the worst-hit countries in West Africa from economic losses linked to the brain drain (Abdeslam, 2008). This phenomenon severely impacted the private sector, which became rife with ponzi schemes that enriched administration officials but led to little economic growth. Furthermore, it created a vacuum in private enterprise development and diminished the prospects of nurturing an entrepreneurship ecosystem. What should have been market-based competition involving capability and skills exploitation and exchanges became a simple metaphor for developing the private sector. Training schemes and programmes that did little for the needs of industry or to sustainably develop an ecosystem became elaborate.

The capital flight that ensued worsened conditions as the cash-choked administration came after private assets through taxation schemes. As a result, many businesses suffered from forced closures or non-voluntary sale of assets, usually to President Jammeh himself. As hard currency earners in the diaspora kept their wealth outside of the country, the scope of remittances reduced, serving mainly to cover living costs. Little else could be set aside as investments, which could have provided a boost to an already failing economy (International Trade Administration, 2018). Corruption squeezed wages for the masses and enriched often-incompetent management executives appointed based on political affiliation and allegiance.

As President Jammeh's administration stepped up its self-preservation efforts, the private sector virtually collapsed and job creation became stagnant. The public sector, which had always been the biggest employer in the country, struggled to maintain wages as the cost of living increased. Demand for jobs in the services sector exceeded the number of jobs available, and it struggled to absorb graduates, while interest in the agricultural sector dwindled as a result of low yields and adverse weather conditions. Tourism continued to provide for many families, but its seasonal nature meant that sustainability within that industry was always lacking. Tapping into foreign labour and expertise became inevitable as key sectors shifted into the hands of workers from the subregion.

Within the education sector, Nigerian and Ghanaian expats dominated the teaching field, while Senegalese skilled labour sought and filled blue-collar jobs. Economic immigrants and foreign consultants were able to secure the few white-collar job opportunities available, often very lucrative, leaving little for the average Gambian to secure a decent livelihood.

Gradually worsening over the Jammeh presidency, by 2016 unemployment among Gambian youth shot up to nearly 60 per cent (GBoS, 2016). In their hunt for prospective income-generating activities, many were pushed to try to start their own businesses, which was in large part influenced by the prevalence of entrepreneurship training programmes (ITC, 2019). Inflated funding from the international donor community for such programmes inundated an already crowded market with service providers that could have benefitted from regional partnerships, value chain development training and support for micro, small and medium-sized enterprises (mSMEs) (UN-DESA, 2019).

With the closure of many initiatives beyond the first to third year of operation, frustration settled in among many young people who began to look for jobs and opportunities elsewhere. Furthermore, the political situation made victims of many young people, as they confronted kidnappings, disappearances and arbitrary arrests of their peers and family members. The attraction of a safer life elsewhere with access to more decent and stable jobs lured many towards clandestine migration through uncertain and dangerous journeys targeting southern Europe as entry points to what they regarded as greener pastures. Radical political change was needed to transform the country, and when the opportunity presented itself in the 2016 presidential elections, the diaspora struck in harmony.

The Political Influence of the Diaspora

In a concerted effort led by a coalition of political parties, the global Gambian diaspora galvanised around the 2016 presidential elections. Approximately $100,000 (GMD 50 million) was raised from Gambians mainly in Western Europe and the United States to support the coalition campaign (CS Monitor, 2018). Diaspora groups were also able to exert pressure on the Jammeh administration through awareness-raising campaigns and fundraising activities in their host countries. Information and communications technology (ICT) and social media platforms facilitated instantaneous exchanges between the diaspora and actors on the ground. Even when Jammeh responded by bringing the telecommunications network to a standstill, the resilience of technology was demonstrated as Gambians found alternative platforms to communicate what was happening in the country to the rest of the world. Software applications such as FireChat and Bridgefy were promoted to bypass regulations introduced by Jammeh's administration. These efforts contributed to sparking the international goodwill that later materialised into action coordinated on the international arena and through ECOWAS in particular.

With the fall of Jammeh, the Gambian diaspora successfully demonstrated the significance of the role it plays in the building up of Gambian society, for which it holds great sensitivity. The success of the coalition still came as a surprise to many, but what was clear was the opportunity the change presented to the diaspora to forge a new relationship with the country. In deciding whether to continue sending remittances, relocate back to the Gambia or invest from afar, the biggest risk the diaspora faced was misjudging the kind of administration Jammeh's successor was going to lead. Exploring the situation on the ground almost became a necessity in this aspect.

The situation inherited by the third republic presented a frontier challenge of the need to revive the private sector (NDP, 2018). The new administration was swift in employing an inclusive approach that involved the diaspora and other actors within the international and donor communities in a new kind of engagement. Under the Ministry of Foreign Affairs, the government established the Migration and Sustainable Development in the Gambia project. This new unit would explore a diaspora strategy and create a global directorate of Gambians in the diaspora, among other activities. More importantly, it created an annual national forum for members of the diaspora to return home and begin a dialogue to chart an engagement framework. Through such platforms, the diaspora exposed their interest in the construction, ICT and trade logistic sectors, as those areas would eventually benefit from the most diaspora capital financing. This process was also aided by the continuation of a best practice by the new administration in meeting with diaspora groups during international state visits. They were usually accompanied by the permanent secretary for investment or representatives from The Gambia Chamber of Commerce and Industry (GCCI) or The Gambia Investment Enterprise Promotion Agency (GIEPA).

The Future Role of the Diaspora

Such initiatives, along with a renaming of the Ministry for Foreign Affairs to the Ministry of Foreign Affairs, International Cooperation, and Gambians Abroad, expressed that outreach to the diaspora or what some politicians referred to as the eighth region of the Gambia was a priority. Therefore, in the aftermath of the success which brought about the political change that had eluded Gambians for many years, the diaspora must also not become complacent. It should continue to strengthen itself across and within networks to create a new profile for itself and ensure the continuation of its participation in national development. They must engage at a deeper level by acknowledging the current evolving context in the Gambia and taking into account the following as part of that process:

The politicisation of young Gambians: This trend started during the Jammeh presidency with 'the green boys and girls' – the youth wing of his political party. Many of those youth ended up with political appointments and did Jammeh's bidding during his time in office. This structure is something that the diaspora can help to improve in a forward-looking approach to identify potential young Gambians with the needed leadership skills to build on the momentum from 2016. It serves to hedge the bet that they placed in President Adama Barrow, whose leadership style is only now becoming clear. To some extent, the diaspora have already begun their outreach efforts to youth through sponsoring high-profile visits to their host countries and expanding the networks of these young leaders.

Security sector reform: Abstaining from visiting the Gambia due to safety concerns is no longer a threat under the new administration. It is becoming more common for diasporans to visit annually and in some cases multiple times per year. But their engagement with initiatives back home should not be pegged to these visits as it is imperative that they become more proactive. Returnees who had been away from the Gambia for many years, some as far back as 1994, are coming back and exploring available markets and business investment opportunities. With the presence of ECOMIG since December 2016, the chances of a coup or domestic unrest have been significantly reduced.

Political reform and ease of regulations: Open access to the Gambian market also brings in diasporans with large savings, who are in a position to make larger-scale investments. With GIEPA leading the way to ease regulations, it is possible to test small-scale solutions to assess the readiness of the market for larger interventions that are still new or untested. These include technology- and non-technology-based solutions, which can drastically transform the job market and how business is conducted in the Gambia. Furthermore, they can improve ICT tools that the diaspora uses to connect to activities and people more efficiently. This trend must continue if the Gambia is to improve the ease of doing business in the country and facilitate greater business registration and job creation (International Trade Administration, 2018).

The aforementioned interventions provide several opportunities for the Gambian diaspora to explore ways they can contribute to the country's development and its ability to harness its demographic dividend. By continuing to engage with the political structures in the home country, diaspora groups are in a unique position to address some of the critical issues still crippling the country, such as illegal migration. Other issues such as the dependency on the public sector and donor-driven development must be challenged with increased private sector–led development. The Gambian economy has suffered greatly from mismanagement and lack of access to workforce-relevant skills to develop the local economy. Re-engaging with the home country provides the diaspora with the opportunity to contribute to local leadership development, in which they must have a stake because of the stability factor it provides. Good leadership will be crucial in the short and medium terms for the development of both political and economic structures of the country. At the backbone of all of this is the resiliency of the education system.

The Gambian diaspora is in a position to effectively contribute to a brain gain and also play a role in the transformation of the country economically. Major investments are needed in the education sector, centrally in K-12 education, but also in technical and vocational education and training (TVET) programmes. Given the diverse range of skill sets required in an economy poised for change, the diaspora must be prepared to return as teachers and administrators and not just see themselves as investors. In pursuing the provision of access to better livelihoods, it is not sustainable to only invest in youth entrepreneurship and ignore other aspects of entrepreneurship ecosystem development. High data costs, overtaxation and lack of access to finance are just some examples of why the situation is so dire for entrepreneurs. The diaspora must therefore find a way to harness and exploit these opportunities in a diversified and balanced way and, in parallel, contribute to the harnessing of the demographic dividend for national development.

The diaspora alone cannot solve the challenges facing the Gambia, but they are part of the human capital base of the country and will continue to be affected by nation-building efforts as stakeholders in that process. Therefore, they should choose to be involved and if need be, ask to be involved. This will ensure that the development that is pursued is strong, resilient and more inclusive. Diasporas are complex networks that need to be further studied and understood, and one area for possible future research derived from this chapter is the need to understand value systems within diasporas and what shapes them. There is a rare chance to build on the opportunity provided by the political change that took place in the Gambia in 2016, which in great part involved the contributions of a distant but always watching and caring diaspora.

References

African Development Bank Group (AfDB). 2016. 'Catalyzing Youth Opportunity across Africa'. Abidjan, Ivory Coast. https://www.afdb.org/fileadmin/uploads/afdb/Images/high_5s/Job_youth_Africa_Job_youth_Africa.pdf.

African Union. 2017. 'AU Roadmap on Harnessing the Demographic Dividend through Investments in Youth'. https://wcaro.unfpa.org/sites/default/files/pub-pdf/AU%20 2017%20DD%20ROADMAP%20Final%20-%20EN.pdf.

Bridgefy. https://www.bridgefy.me/.

CS Monitor. 2018. 'Gambia's Diaspora Helped Oust a Dictator. Now They're Asking: What's Next?' https://www.csmonitor.com/World/Africa/2018/0129/Gambia-s-diaspora-helped-oust-a-dictator.-Now-they-re-asking-What-s-next.

ECOWAS. 2016. 'ECOWAS, African Union and UN Statement on the Political Developments in the Gambia'. https://www.ecowas.int/ecowas-african-union-and-un-statement-on-the-political-developments-in-the-gambia/.

Faal, Jojoh, and Jonathan Mitchell. 2008. 'The Gambia Tourist Value Chain and Prospects for Pro-Poor Tourism'. Overseas Development Institute (ODI), London.

FireChat. https://www.opengarden.com/firechat/.

Gambia Bureau of Statistics (GBoS). 2016. Integrated Household Survey, 2015/2016.

International Fund for Agricultural Development (IFAD). 2017. 'Sending Money Home: Contributing to the SDGs, One Family at a Time'. https://www.ifad.org/documents/38714170/39135645%20/Sending+Money+Home+-+Contributing+to+the+SDGs%2C+one+family+at+a+time.pdf/c207b5f1-9fef-4877-9315-75463fccfaa7.

International Trade Administration, US Department of Commerce. 2018. Country Commercial Guide: The Gambia. https://legacy.export.gov/article?series=a0pt00000000GtZAAU&type=Country_Commercial__kav.

International Trade Center (ITC). 2019. 'Entrepreneurship Ecosystem in the Gambia: A Network Analysis of Institutions Supporting Entrepreneurship'. https://www.yep.gm/storage/app/uploads/public/5df/390/fd4/5df390fd4f2fe746827579.pdf.

Marfouk, Abdeslam. 2008. 'The African Brain Drain: Scope and Determinants'. DULBEA Working Papers 08-07.RS, ULB – Universite Libre de Bruxelles.

Migration and Sustainable Development in the Gambia. http://gambiandiaspora.net/.

Migration Policy. 2018. 'How Governments Strengthen Ties with Their Diasporas'. https://www.migrationpolicy.org/sites/default/files/publications/Intro_CtD.pdf.

National Development Plan (NDP). 2018. 'Government of the Gambia'. http://ndp.gm/.

Ofuho, Cirino Hiteng. 2009. 'Africa: Teaching IR Where It's Not Supposed to Be'. In Arlene B. Tickner and Ole Waever (eds), *International Relations Scholarship around the World*. Abingdon: Routledge, 71–85.

Ul Haque, Nadeem, and Se-Jik Kim. 1994. 'Human Capital Flight: Impact of Migration on Income and Growth (December 1994)'. IMF Working Paper 94/155, vol., pp. 1–40. https://ssrn.com/abstract=883914.

UN-DESA. 2019. 'Enhancing National Capacities for Unleashing Full Potentials of Micro-, Small and Medium Enterprises (MSMEs) in Achieving the Sustainable Development Goals (SDGs) in the Gambia'. New York.

UNDP. 2019. 'Scaling Fences: Voices of Irregular African Migrants to Europe'. https://www.undp.org/content/undp/en/home/librarypage/democratic-governance/ScalingFences.html.

US Department of Commerce. 2019. 'Country Commercial Guide, the Gambia'. https://www.export.gov/article?id=Gambia-Market-Overview.

Youth Empowerment Project (YEP). 2019. International Trade Center (ITC). https://yep.gm/.

References on Landscape Review of Diaspora

Ács, Z. J. 2006. 'How Is Entrepreneurship Good for Economic Growth?' *Innovations*, 1, 96–107.

Agunias, D. R., and K. Newland. 2012. 'Developing a Road Map for Engaging Diasporas in Development: A Handbook for Policymakers and Practitioners in Home and Host Countries'. Geneva, Switzerland: International Organization for Migration.

Åkesson, L. 2015. 'Obstacles and Openings: Returnees and Small-Scale Businesses in Cape Verde'. In L. Åkesson and M. Eriksson Baaz (eds), *Africa's Return Migrants: The New Developers?*, pp. 152–72. London: Zed Books.

Åkesson, L., and M. Eriksson Baaz. 2015. 'Introduction'. In L. Åkesson and M. Eriksson Baaz (eds), *Africa's Return Migrants: The New Developers?*, pp. 1–22. London: Zed Books.

Ammassari, S. 2004. 'From Nation-Building to Entrepreneurship: The Impact of Élite Return Migrants in Côte d'Ivoire and Ghana'. *Population, Space and Place* 10(2), 133–54.

Anderloni, L., and D. Vandone. 2008a. 'Migrants and Financial Services'. Paper as part of the 'Financial Services Provision and Prevention of Financial Exclusion', study commissioned by the European Commission, Employment, Social Affairs and Equal Opportunities DG, under the study service contract reference no. EC/2006/0183. Retrieved 5 March 2019. http://www.ecosocdoc.be/static/module/BIBLIOGRAPHYDocument/document/001/377.pdf.

———. 2008b. 'Migrants and Financial Services: Which Opportunities for Financial Innovation?' In P. Molyneux and E. Vallelado (eds), *Frontiers of Banks in a Global Economy*, pp. 149–85. London: Palgrave Macmillan.

Atkinson, A., and F. A. Messy. 2015. 'Financial Education for Migrants and Their Families'. OECD Working Papers on Finance, Insurance and Private Pensions, no. 38. Paris: OECD Publishing. http://dx.doi.org/10.1787/5js4h5rw17vh-en.

Beine, M., F. Docquier and C. Özden. 2011. 'Diasporas'. *Journal of Development Economics* 95(1), 30–41.

Beine, M., F. Docquier and H. Rapoport. 2008. 'Brain Drain and Human Capital Formation in Developing Countries: Winners and Losers'. *Economic Journal* 118(528), 631–52.

Bhagwati, J., and K. Hamada. 1974. 'The Brain Drain, International Integration of Markets for Professionals and Unemployment: A Theoretical Analysis'. *Journal of Development Economics* 1(1), 19–42.

Bilgili, Ö., and M. Siegel. 2017. 'To Return Permanently or to Return Temporarily? Explaining Migrants' Intentions'. *Migration and Development* 6(1), 14–32.

Black, R., and A. Castaldo. 2009. 'Return Migration and Entrepreneurship in Ghana and Côte d'Ivoire: The Role of Capital Transfers'. *Tijdschrift voor economische en sociale geografie* 100(1), 44–58.

Black, R., R. King and R. Tiemoko. 2003. 'Migration, Return and Small Enterprise Development in Ghana: A Route Out of Poverty'. International Workshop on Migration and Poverty in West Africa. Sussex, UK: University of Sussex.

Brinkerhoff, J. 2008. 'The Potential of Diasporas and Development'. In J. Brinkerhoff (ed.), *Diasporas and Development*, pp. 1–15. Boulder, CO: Rienner.

Carling, J., M. Bolognani, M. B. Erdal, R. T. Ezzat, C. Oeppen, E. Paasche, S. V. Pettersen and T. H. Sagmo. 2015. *Possibilities and Realities of Return Migration*. Oslo, Norway: Peace Research Institute Oslo (PRIO).

Castles, S., and M. J. Miller. 1993. *The Age of Migration: International Population Movements in the Modern World.* London: Macmillan.

Chetail, V. 2012. 'Sources of International Migration Law'. In B. Opeskin, R. Perruchoud and J. Redpath-Cross (eds), *Foundations of International Migration Law*, pp. 56–92. New York: Cambridge University Press.

Clydesdale, G. 2008. 'Business Immigrants and the Entrepreneurial Nexus'. *Journal of International Entrepreneurship* 6, 123–42.

Collier, P., and A. Hoeffler. 2004. 'Greed and Grievance in Civil War'. *Oxford Economic Papers* 56(4), 563–95.

Collier, W., M. Piracha and T. Randazzo. 2011. 'Remittances and Return Migration'. *Comparative Political Studies* 50(1), 75–101.

Dalziel, M. 2008. 'Immigrants as Extraordinarily Successful Entrepreneurs: A Pilot Study of the Canadian Experience'. *Journal of Small Business & Entrepreneurship* 21(1), 23–36.

De Haas, H. 2005. 'International Migration, Remittances and Development: Myths and Facts'. *Third World Quarterly* 26(8), 1269–84.

———. 2006. 'Engaging Diasporas – How Governments and Development Agencies Can Support Diaspora Involvement in the Development of Their Origin Countries'. Oxford, UK: International Migration Institute (IMI), University of Oxford.

———. 2010. 'Migration and Development: A Theoretical Perspective'. *International Migration Review* 44(1), 227–64.

Di Giovanni, J., A. A. Levchenko and F. Ortega. 2015. 'A Global View of Cross-Border Migration'. *Journal of European Economic Association* 13(1), 168–202.

Docquier, F., and H. Rapoport. 2012. 'Globalization, Brain Drain, and Development'. *Journal of Economic Literature* 50(3), 681–730.

Drori, I., B. Honig and M. Wright. 2009. 'Transnational Entrepreneurship: An Emergent Field of Study'. *Entrepreneurship Theory and Practice* 33(5), 1001–22.

EIB. 2006. 'Study on Improving the Efficiency of Workers' Remittances in Mediterranean Countries'. Rotterdam, the Netherlands: European Investment Bank. Retrieved 6 March 2019. http://www.eib.org/attachments/country/femip_workers_remittances_en.pdf.

Elo, M. 2016. 'Typology of Diaspora Entrepreneurship: Case Studies in Uzbekistan'. *Journal of International Entrepreneurship* 14(1), 121–55.

Elo, M., et al. 2018. 'Advancing the Views on Migrant and Diaspora Entrepreneurs in International Entrepreneurship'. *Journal of International Entrepreneurship* 16(2), 119–33.

Eriksson Baaz, M. 2015. 'Successive Flops and Occasional Feats: Development Contributions and Thorny Social Navigation among Congolese Return Migrants'. In L. Åkesson and M. Eriksson Baaz (eds), *Africa's Return Migrants: The New Developers?*, pp. 23–43. London: Zed Books.

Famoroti, M. 2018. 'Foresight Africa Viewpoint – Debt by Diaspora: Ties That Bond'. Washington, DC: Brookings Institution. Retrieved 20 December 2018. https://www.brookings.edu/blog/africa-in-focus/2018/01/24/foresight-africa-viewpoint-debt-by-diaspora-ties-that-bond/.

Ferrantide, D., and A. J. Ody. 2007. 'What Can Remittances and Other Migrant Flows Do for Equitable Development?' In B. J. Merz, L. C. Chen and P. F. Geithner (eds), *Diasporas and Development. Global Equity Initiative*, pp. 55–88. Cambridge, MA: Harvard University Press.

Fransen, S., and V. Mazzucatto. 2014. 'Remittances and Household Wealth after Conflict: A Case Study on Urban Burundi'. *World Development* 60, 57–68.

Fransen, S., and M. Siegel. 2011. 'The Development of Diaspora Engagement Policies in Burundi and Rwanda'. UNU-MERIT Working Paper no. 2011–038. Maastricht, the Netherlands: Maastricht Graduate School of Governance (MGSoG).

Fransen, S., I. Ruiz and C. Vargas-Silva. 2017. 'Return Migration and Economic Outcomes in the Conflict Context'. *World Development* 95, 196–210.

Gamlen, A. 2014. 'The New Migration-and-Development Pessimism'. *Progress in Human Geography* 38(4), 581–97.

Gillespie, K., L. Riddle, E. Sayre and D. Sturges. 1999. 'Diaspora Interest in Homeland Investment'. *Journal of International Business Studies* 30(3), 623–34.

Goldring, L. 2004. 'Family and Collective Remittances to Mexico: A Multidimensional Typology'. *Development and Change* 35(4), 799–840.

Grabska, K. 2014. *Gender, Identity and Home: Nuer Repatriation to Southern Sudan*. Martlesham: James Curry.

Hanafi, S. 2008. 'Modes of Entrepreneurship of Palestinian Refugees in the Palestinian Territory: Camps versus Cities of the West Bank'. CARIM Analytic and Synthetic Notes 2008/45.

Hunger, U. 2002. 'The "Brain Gain" Hypothesis: Third-World Elites in Industrialized Countries and Socioeconomic Development in Their Home Country'. Working Paper 47. Muenster, Germany: Center for Comparative Immigration Studies, University of Muenster.

IFRC. 2009. 'International Federation of Red Cross and Red Crescent Societies' (IFRC) Policy on Migration'. Geneva, Switzerland: International Committee of the Red Cross and Red Crescent Societies.

———. 2017. 'IFRC Global Strategy on Migration 2018–2022: Reducing Vulnerability, Enhancing Resilience'. Geneva, Switzerland: International Committee of the Red Cross and Red Crescent Societies.

ILO. 2006. ILO Multilateral Framework on Labour Migration: Non-binding Principles and Guidelines for a Rights-Based Approach to Labour Migration'. Geneva, Switzerland: International Labour Organization.

Jones, R. C. 1998. 'Introduction: The Renewed Role of Remittances in the New World Order'. *Economic Geography* 74(1), 1–7.

Ketkar, S. L., and D. Ratha. 2007. 'Development Finance via Diaspora Bonds Track Record and Potential'. Paper presented at the Migration and Development Conference at the World Bank on 23 May 2007, Washington, DC: World Bank.

———. 2011. 'Diaspora Bonds: Tapping the Diaspora during Difficult Times'. In S. Plaza and D. Ratha (eds), *Diaspora for Development in Africa*, pp. 127–44. Washington, DC: World Bank.

Kotabe, M., L. Riddle, P. Sonderegger and F. A. Täube. 2013. 'Diaspora Investment and Entrepreneurship: The Role of People, Their Movements, and Capital in the International Economy'. *Journal of International Management* 19(1), 3–5.

Kourtit, K., and P. Nijkamp. 2018. 'Educational Migrants: A Special Type of Cross-Border Migration'. *Cross-Border Journal for International Studies* 2(3).

Kuschminder K., G. Sturge and N. Ragab. 2014. 'Contributions and Barriers to Knowledge Transfer: The Experience of Returning Experts'. CIM Paper Series 7. Eschborn, Germany: Centre for International Migration and Development.

Leblang, D. 2017. 'Harnessing the Diaspora: Dual Citizenship, Migrant Return Remittances'. *Comparative Political Studies* 50(1), 75–101.

Levitt, P. 1998. 'Social Remittances: Migration Driven Local-Level Forms of Cultural Diffusion'. *International Migration Review* 32(4), 926–48.

Levitt, P., and D. Lamba-Nieves. 2010. 'Social Remittances Revisited'. *Journal of Ethnic and Migration Studies* 37(1), 1–22.

Light, I., and S. Gold. 2000. *Ethnic Economies*. San Diego, CA: Academic Press.

Lin, X., and S. Tao. 2012. 'Transnational Entrepreneurs: Characteristics, Drivers, and Success Factors'. *Journal of International Entrepreneurship* 10(1), 50–69.

Lundberg, H., and A. Rehnfors. 2018. 'Transnational Entrepreneurship: Opportunity Identification and Venture Creation'. *Journal of International Entrepreneurship* 16(2), 150–75.

Mambula, C. J., and F. E. Sawyer. 2004. 'Acts of Entrepreneurial Creativity for Business Growth and Survival in a Constrained Economy'. *International Journal of Social Economics* 31(1/2), 30–55.

Marchand, K., S. Fransen and M. Siegel. 2013. 'Migrant Entrepreneurship, Remittances & Development'. Background Paper International Policy Debate, 29 May 2013. Maastricht, the Netherlands: United Nations University-MERIT (UNU-MERIT)/ Maastricht Graduate School of Governance (MGSoG).

Mascini, P., A. Fermin and H. Snick. 2012. 'Transnationalism of Burundian Refugees in The Netherlands: The Importance of Migration Motives'. *International Journal of Population Research*, 1–11.

Massey, D. S., J. Arango, G. Hugo, A. Kouaouci, A. Pellegrino and J. E. Taylor. 1998. *Worlds in Motion: Understanding International Migration at the End of the Millennium*. Oxford, UK: Clarendon Press.

McCormick, B., and J. Wahba. 2001. 'Overseas Work Experience, Savings and Entrepreneurship amongst Return Migrants to LDCs'. *Scottish Journal of Political Economy* 48(2), 164–78.

Meyer, J. B., and M. Brown. 1999. 'Scientific Diasporas: A New Approach to the Brain Drain'. Paper presented at the 'World Conference on Science' UNESCO-ICSU, Budapest, 26 June–1 July 1999. Accessed 13 December 2018. https://unesdoc.unesco.org/ark:/48223/pf0000116330.

Mohamoud, A., and C. Formson-Lorist. 2014. 'Diaspora and Migrant Entrepreneurs as Social and Economic Investors in Homeland Development'. The Hague, the Netherlands: African Diaspora Policy Centre.

Naudé, W., M. Siegel and K. Marchand. 2015. 'Migration, Entrepreneurship and Development: A Critical Review'. IZA Discussion Paper Series no. 9284. Bonn, Germany: Institute for the Study of Labor (IZA).

———. 2017. 'Migration, Entrepreneurship and Development: Critical Questions'. *IZA Journal of Migration* 6(5), 1–16.

Nevinskaitė, L. 2016. 'Social Remittances from the Professional Diaspora: The Issue of Home-Country Receptivity'. *Central and Eastern European Migration Review* 5(2), 135–53.

Newland, K. 2010. 'Six Studies and a Road Map: Diasporas as Partners in Development'. In K. Newland (ed.), *Diasporas: New Partners in Global Development Policy*, pp. 1–24. Washington, DC: MPI.

Newland, K., and H. Tanaka. 2010. *Mobilizing Diaspora Entrepreneurship for Development*. Washington, DC: Migration Policy Institute.

Nielsen, T. M., and L. Riddle. 2010. 'Investing in Peace: The Motivational Dynamics of Diaspora Investment in Postconflict Economies'. *Journal of Business Ethics* 89, 435–48.

Nkongolo-Bakenda, J.-M., and E. V. Chrysostome. 2013. 'Engaging Diasporas as International Entrepreneurs in Developing Countries: In Search of Determinants'. *Journal of International Entrepreneurship* 11(1), 30–64.

Nyberg-Sørensen, N. 2004. 'The Development Dimension of Migrant Remittances'. Migration Policy Research Working Paper Series, no. 1, Geneva, Switzerland: International Organization of Migration.

Nyberg-Sørensen, N., and K. Fog Olwig. 2002. *Work and Migration: Life and Livelihoods in a Globalizing World*. London: Routledge.

Nyberg-Sørensen, N. N., N. Van Hear and P. Engberg-Pedersen. 2002. 'The Migration-Development Nexus: Evidence and Policy Options State-of-the-Art Overview'. *International Migration* 40(5), 1–47.

Oddou, G., B. Szkudlarek, J. S. Osland, J. Deller, R. Blakeney and N. Furuya. 2013. 'Repatriates as a Source of Competitive Advantage: How to Manage Knowledge Transfer'. *Organizational Dynamics* 42(4), 257–66.

OECD. 2017. 'Interrelations between Public Policies, Migration and Development'. Paris, France: Organisation for Economic Co-operation and Development.

Page, J., and S. Plaza. 2006. 'Migration Remittances and Development: A Review of Global Evidence'. *Journal of African Economies* 15(suppl. 2), 245–336.

Portes, A. 2003. 'Conclusion: Theoretical Convergencies and Empirical Evidence in the Study of Immigrant Transnationalism'. *International Migration Review* 37(3), 874–92.

Portes, A., W. J. Haller and L. E. Guarnizo. 2002. 'Transnational Entrepreneurs: An Alternative Form of Immigrant Economic Adaptation'. *American Sociological Review* 67(2), 278–98.

Pruthi, S., A. Basu and M. Wright. 2018. 'Ethnic Ties, Motivations, and Home Country Entry Strategy of Transnational Entrepreneurs'. *Journal of International Entrepreneurship* 16(2), 210–43.

Putnam, R. D. 2000. *Bowling Alone*. New York: Free Press.

Riddle, L. 2008. 'Diasporas: Exploring Their Development Potential'. *Journal of Microfinance/ESR Review* 10(2), 28–35.

Riddle, L., and J. Brinkerhoff. 2011. 'Diaspora Entrepreneurs as Institutional Change Agents: The Case of Thamel.com'. *International Business Review* 20, 670–80.

Sagmo, T. H. 2015. 'The Role of Social Capital in Post-Conflict Business Development: Perspectives from Returning Migrants in Burundi'. In L. Åkesson and M. Eriksson Baaz (eds), *Africa's Return Migrants: The New Developers?*, pp. 109–29. London: Zed Books.

Sana, M. 2005. 'Buying Membership in the Transnational Community: Migrant Remittances, Social Status and Assimilation'. *Population Research and Policy Review* 24, 231–61.

Saxenian, A. 2002. Brain Circulation: How High-Skill Immigration Makes Everyone Better Off'. *Brookings Review* 20(1), 28–31.

Schumpeter, J. 1942. *Capitalism, Socialism and Democracy*. London: Harper & Brothers.

Sheffer, G. 1986. 'A New Field of Study: Modern Diasporas in International Politics'. In G. Sheffer (eds), *Modern Diasporas in International Politics*, pp. 1–15. London: Croom Helm.

Sims, R. H., and M. Schraeder. 2004. 'An Examination of Salient Factors Affecting Expatriate Culture Shock'. *Journal of Business Management* 10(1), 73–87.

Stefansson, A. 2004. 'Homecomings to the Future: From Diasporic Mythographies to Social Projects of Return'. In F. Markowitz and A. Stefansson (eds), *Homecomings: Unsettling Paths of Return*, pp. 2–20. Lanham, MD: Lexington Books.

Stel, N. 2013. 'Diaspora versus Refugee – The Political Economy of Lebanese Entrepreneurship Regimes'. Maastricht School of Management Working Paper no. 16/2013. Maastricht, the Netherlands: Maastricht School of Management.

Taylor, J. E. 1999. 'The New Economics of Labour Migration and the Role of Remittances in the Migration Process'. *International Migration* 37(1), 63–88.

Tiemoko, R. 2004. 'Unveiling Local Opportunities and Challenges in Return Migration and Development Nexus: The Case of Côte d'Ivoire and Ghana'. Brighton, UK: University of Sussex, Sussex Centre for Migration Research.

Trans, L. O., and I. M. Vammen. 2011. 'African Diaspora Associations in Denmark: A Study of Their Development Activities and Potentials'. In S. Plaza and D. Ratha (eds), *Diaspora for Development in Africa*, pp. 145–64. Washington, DC: World Bank.

UNDP. 2011. Towards Human Resilience: Sustaining MDG Progress in an Age of Economic Uncertainty. New York, NY: United Nations Development Programme.

USAID. 2009. 'Diaspora Direct Investment (DDI): The Untapped Resource for Development'. Washington, DC: US Agency for International Development. http://pdf.usaid.gov/pdf_docs/PNADO983.pdf.

Vaaler, P. M. 2011. 'Immigrant Remittances and the Venture Investment Environment of Developing Countries'. *Journal of International Business Studies* 42(9), 1121–49.

———. 2013. 'Diaspora Concentration and the Venture Investment Impact of Remittances'. *Journal of International Management* 19(1), 26–46.

Vemuri, S. R. 2014. 'Formation of Diaspora Entrepreneurs'. ZenTra Working Papers in Transnational Studies 41/2014. Bremen, Germany: ZenTra Center for Transnational Studies.

Wahba, J., and Y. Zenou. 2012. 'Out of Sight, Out of Mind: Migration, Entrepreneurship and Social Capital'. *Regional Science and Urban Economics* 42(5), 890–903.

Yang, D. 2011. 'Migrant Remittances'. *Journal of Economic Perspectives* 25(3), 129–51.

Chapter 4

ENGAGING YOUTH TO ADDRESS SEXUAL VIOLENCE IN INDIA

ElsaMarie D'Silva

> Last month, I was sexually assaulted on my college campus by a man [...] I can vividly recall that at the happenstance of the incident, there were nine seconds of processing what I went through. I remember gathering up all my courage, running and informing the guards. And we caught hold of the man.
>
> Although I felt very brave throughout the entire period for taking action, I cannot ever forget those few nine seconds which back then seemed like an eternity of me debating what to do over and over again, whether to take a stand for myself or just to ignore it. And I must tell you this, all the Safecity workshops went in a flash before me in those pivotal nine seconds that I realised it was the time for me to practise what I had been preaching. I want to thank you from the bottom of my heart for believing in the 18-year-old me, two years ago. Hadn't it been for Safecity, I might have dealt with this incident very differently.
>
> – Email from A.S., 29 March 2019

This was an email I received last year from a young woman who had started off as a volunteer and then joined the team of the NGO I run as a programme officer. At the time, she was studying for her master's programme at a premier college in Mumbai, India. The email was extremely moving and brought tears to my eyes because helping people like her who know their rights and options for dealing with harassment is exactly the essence of our work at Red Dot Foundation (Safecity). We work tirelessly to make public spaces safer for women and girls through education, crowdsourced data and community engagement.

Sexual violence is a global pandemic, and in India, it is a barrier to women's empowerment. According to the National Crime Records Bureau (NCRB, 2018, p. 7), a rape occurs somewhere in India every 18 minutes. This violence has taken a toll on the physical, psychological and economic development of women and girls. The McKinsey Global Institute's 'Power of Parity: Advancing Women's Equality in Asia Pacific' report (2018) states that in a best-case scenario, India could add US$770 billion to its GDP if it succeeded in advancing women's equality. Violence against women and girls was listed as one of the barriers that prevented this advancement.

As we have seen in our work, sexual violence has been normalised to such an extent that many young girls are not even aware of it being inappropriate or a crime. As a result, they often do not speak up or officially report the incident. Research by Girija Borker (2018, p. 1) using the Safecity data found that women in Delhi compromised on the quality of their education by choosing a college nearer their homes as they did not feel safe travelling. Further, she estimated that they were willing to spend an additional US$290 or INR 18,000 per year on transport options and routes that were safer. This additional amount translated to equal or double the amount spent on tuition and was unlike that spent by their male counterparts.

Therefore, when discussing the potential of India's demographic dividend, it is important to take into account the creation of an enabling and safe environment for young girls to get a proper education and enter the workforce.

India has one of the youngest populations in the world with over 60 per cent of its 1.3 billion people in the age group of 15–59 years. This is expected to peak around 2036 when this age group will comprise about 65 per cent of the population (Singh, 2018). According to 2020 statistics, the median age in India is 28, compared to 37 in China and the United States, 45 in Western Europe and 49 in Japan, making the Indian demographic the labour force of the world (Ghani, 2018). However, Jaffrelot and Kalyankar (2019) believe that the country has reached its peak of under-19-year-olds and is in a position to maximise the demographic dividend if focus on education and skilling is given priority.

According to the United Nations Population Fund (UNFPA, n.d.), a demographic dividend means 'the economic growth potential that can result from shifts in a population's age structure, mainly when the share of the working-age population (15 to 64) is larger than the non-working-age share of the population (14 and younger, and 65 and older)'.

On paper, this concept sounds great. Countries like Japan have in the past benefitted from this phenomenon where they experienced rapid growth between 1964 and 2004, due to a changing population structure (Ft.com, 2012). This results in increased productivity driven by an increased labour force, a rise in the number of women in the formal workforce due to declining fertility and increased financial resources due to spending and savings. There is an overall uptick in the economy due to higher economic activities leading to rapid industrialisation and urbanisation with large numbers of people seeking employment.

A Need for Civic and Social Skills

In reality, a country can maximise the full potential of the dividend if there is focused intentionality in policymaking that can leverage this exact period of time when a particular demographic can make its highest contribution to the economy and the overall gross domestic product (GDP) of the country. It means that there should be nuanced policymaking that is set in visionary planning and implementation of schemes and programmes to realise the socio-economic benefit of the population. This will require investments in health and education schemes and infrastructure, gender equality, reduction in violence against women and girls and effective job creation as these are essential to achieving the demographic dividend.

The United Nations Sustainable Development Goal (SDG) 4 is 'quality education', which is to ensure inclusive and equitable quality education and promote lifelong learning opportunities for all. It further emphasises that

> education liberates the intellect, unlocks the imagination and is fundamental for self-respect. It is the key to prosperity and opens a world of opportunities, making it possible for each of us to contribute to a progressive, healthy society. Learning benefits every human being and should be available to all. (Global Goals, n.d.)

Linking SDG4 with other SDGs such as 'gender equality' (SDG5) and 'reduced inequality' (SDG10) is the need of the hour. Not only should everyone have the right to education, which is now a law in India (Mhrd.gov.in, 2019), but also access to quality education that includes values. It is important to ensure young people have the self-confidence and self-esteem to avail of opportunities in education and careers and further their financial independence.

However, there is concern that India might miss the opportunity in this period and not fully leverage its potential because its education system is not consistent. Graduating students are excellent at rote learning, but often cannot think critically or develop their creative abilities and certainly do not have the requisite skills to be job ready for the market's needs. Further, the education system does not cover curricula on sex education and healthy relationships as these are considered taboo when in fact it would give them the information required to deal with reality. Many have likened the educational system to a factory model churning out clerks to meet the needs of the Industrial

Revolution of the eighteenth and nineteenth centuries, which is not relevant to current times (Ramya, 2012).

On one hand, there are premier institutions like the Indian Institutes of Technology (IITs) and Indian Institutes of Management (IIMs) that produce elite students in engineering and management, while on the other, there are millions of young people who are deprived of quality education because of the lack of basics in the form of teachers and infrastructure. In the QS World University Rankings 2019, only three Indian universities were featured in the top 200 (Top Universities, n.d.).

According to the SDG India Index Baseline Report 2018, India's performance on SDG4 is average with a score of about 50 per cent (Niti.gov.in, 2018); 13 states reported above-average performance on selected indicators while 9 performed at average and 7 at below-average levels. The state government of Delhi has recently introduced a Happiness Curriculum which is based on a strong humanitarian and social need. It includes value-based curricula and meditation, and it will be interesting to see its impact in a few years.

Therefore, there is a need to urgently address the gaps in the education system and complement the curriculum with activities and life skills training to transform youth active contributors to a democratic society. Further, there is a lack of emphasis in developing social skills such as respect and empathy or advanced civic skills such as rights-based education. It is problematic if half a billion people or more are working in suboptimal conditions, without the necessary skill sets or opportunities. Building confidence and leadership is essential in developing the capacity of youth to take charge and be agents of change. I've seen this first-hand in my work.

Mapping Sexual Violence

When my friends and I started Safecity in December 2012, we believed in creating a people's movement to address the issue of sexual violence. The platform Safecity was launched in response to the horrific gang rape of Jyoti Singh on a bus in Delhi. It was a brutal incident which cost Jyoti her life and was an inflection point in youth activism where many took to the streets to protest and demand accountability. Capitalising on this momentum for change, we launched Safecity, a platform to report anonymous stories and experiences of sexual violence in public spaces. The aim was to understand location-based patterns and trends to facilitate localised solutions. Since then, we have crowdsourced the largest number of stories in the world with the largest datasets being from India and Kenya (Figure 4.1) (Safecity.in, n.d.).

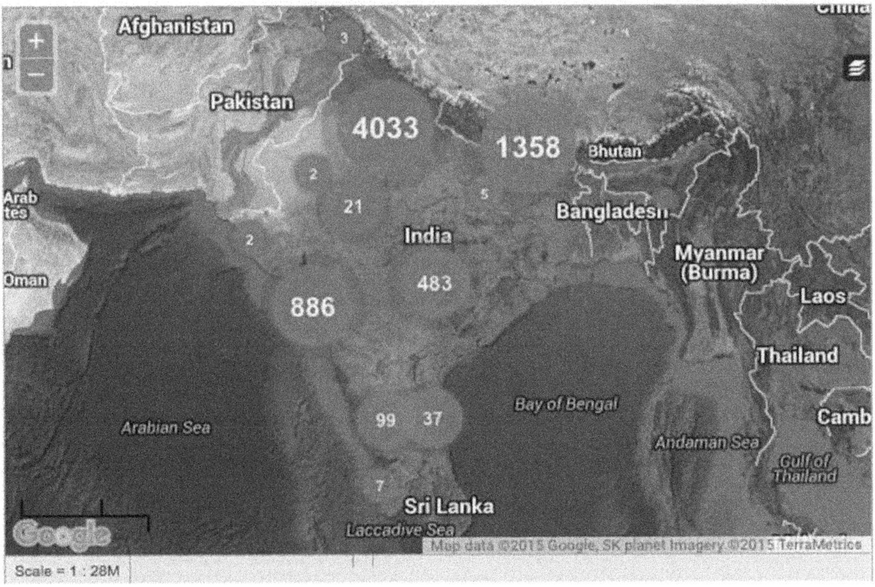

Figure 4.1 Zoomed in map of Safecity. Credit: ElsaMarie D'Silva.

From the very start, we engaged youth as volunteers to be agents of change. We invited them to work with us in their communities and on college campuses as campus ambassadors (CAs). Over a six-month period, we trained them to be peer educators, encouraging fellow students about the spectrum of abuse and the various legislations in effect that protect their rights, the formal redressal mechanisms and ways Safecity could be useful. By accessing the open-sourced data on the Safecity platform, they could begin a dialogue with their peers and involve the larger community in finding solutions.

For example, many young people – men and women – did not fully understand the issue of sexual violence. At each of our workshops on sexual violence, which we hold on college campuses, we ask students to indicate with a show of hands if they have *never* experienced any form of sexual violence, and often several of them raise their hands. We then go through the definitions and the forms of sexual violence and ask for a show of hands once again, and then, not surprisingly, not a single hand goes up.

Having access to data is critical as most crimes are under-reported and often sexual violence that falls in the verbal and non-verbal categories are not reported as the victim thinks it is too trivial to report, or it has become normalised over a period of time. One of the first projects that we worked on was with five youth volunteers of Guru Gobind Singh Indraprastha University in the Dwarka area of Delhi. The students shared their personal experiences of sexual violence in public spaces and wanted to make their college campus and surroundings safer. Their mobility and access to these spaces was hindered by various social, systemic and infrastructural elements which made it unsafe, especially for female students. They reached out to over three hundred students who were further engaged to understand the importance of reporting incidents of sexual violence and understanding sexual harassment rights and laws. Through street plays and street audits, they reached out to another two thousand people in the area with surveys and identified hotspots and broken infrastructure like non-functional streetlights.

The process of building data allowed them to see the deficits of public spaces in terms of infrastructure and police surveillance, the emerging concept of gated communities, the scattered development of Dwarka and poor lighting in most pockets of the place. One of the hotspots was the metro station of Dwarka Mor. Within a week of submitting the sexual harassment reports, the metro officials started monitoring entries and exits into the metro station and had repaired the non-functioning lights around the station. The metro guards also started regulating the crowd around the metro station, especially drivers of autos and rickshaws parked for extended hours. The campaign team spoke to the commuters over a two-day period after the intervention and concluded with a majority opinion stating that they felt safer accessing this metro station (Safecity.in, 2015).

Interventions such as these in communities and college campuses and around railway stations have resulted in an increase in confidence among the youth after engaging with institutional stakeholders such as the police, railway officials and municipal authorities. Through a focused programme on gender sensitisation and leadership programme on college campuses, we can engage youth to contribute towards change through personal reflection and being peer educators and innovators.

The Value of Volunteering

In her exit interview Renita Sequeira, who was our communications officer, shared her experience:

> I had just completed my graduation and was, in a way, living in a cocoon or a more protected environment. I was aware of the serious lack of safety that women face but I didn't know whether or how I could do anything about it. As an individual, I have become more aware of societal norms, inequalities, injustice. I now

> know that I don't have to accept them, and I've learned to voice my opinions against them. I am no longer as apathetic or ignorant to the situation around me as I used to be. I have grown in confidence in myself and my skills. Safecity has taught me to embrace new experiences and to learn from them.

Over the past seven years, we have worked with over five hundred youth. Of the CAs we worked with, 80% said their leadership was greatly enhanced while 95 per cent said they have a better understanding about sexual violence and strategies for prevention and 92 per cent felt they are more likely now to take action (Safecity.in, 2017).

Tanuja Nailwal, one of our Delhi volunteers and a CA, reported of her stint with us in an email:

> Non-profits like Safecity allows us students to do their bit in different capacities thus fulfilling their desires and giving them the inner mental peace. Not only this, volunteering enhances a student's skills set, network and knowledge of the on-ground realities. Education can give you the theoretical knowledge but only through its application can one realise the implication and implementation of that experience, and I believe volunteering to be the essence of such an experience. Empathy is another trait which volunteering fills you with because you work on issues which will ultimately have an impact on another person.

Vanshika Deswal, another youth volunteer, said in an email:

> It's my fourth year with Safecity and I can never imagine myself not working with it. I am a more confident, brave version of myself apart from being more empathetic and understanding. Having dealt with major self-esteem issues throughout my school life, it's because of all the platforms that Safecity provided me that I was able to overcome that. Since the issue (sexual violence) is not independent of politics, economy or technology, I have learnt so much about these subjects as well. This may sound egoistic, but I believe this knowledge gives me an edge over my peers in terms of career opportunities.

Another way we engage young people is through volunteering opportunities as data analysts or bloggers and social media experts. Many young men volunteer to analyse the data which helps them understand the issue and become more empathetic. One of our first data analysts was shocked to learn that the peak of sexual harassment experienced by women in India was between noon and 2:00 p.m. It was only when he understood that we were mapping sexual violence in public spaces and most women return home from work and other activities by dusk that he realised he needed to educate himself further on this topic.

Vihang Jumle, another young male volunteer and data analyst, said in an email:

> As an individual, I have only become more mature and sensitive to gender differences (since working with Safecity). I have become aware of how sexual crimes affect people and why it is important to do something about it. I now heed elements such as inclusivity, social etiquettes, consent, etc. in things that I pursue. I think I have also become more empathetic.

Engaging men and boys in this issue is a game changer. Often, sexual violence is treated as a woman's issue when in truth it is a societal one. As is seen in Figure 4.2, community dialogues are important in helping men and boys understand their privilege and address the norms of toxic masculinity. We can thus increase empathy and bring more harmony between the genders.

Changing cultures of violence are partly about policies, but it is also about giving people a voice. The importance of creating platforms for youth to

Figure 4.2 Youth volunteers in Delhi. Credit: Red Dot Foundation.

learn life skills by 'doing' and having the opportunity to 'fail' while being able to experiment on solutions for social issues is critical in a vibrant and active democracy.

References

Borker, G. 2018. 'Safety First: Perceived Risk of Street Harassment and Educational Choices of Women' (online). Available at: https://data2x.org/wp-content/uploads/2019/11/PerceivedRiskStreetHarassmentandEdChoicesofWomen_Borker.pdf.

Edudel.nic.in. 2019. 'Happiness Curriculum' (online). Available at: http://www.edudel.nic.in/welcome_folder/happiness/HappinessCurriculumFramework_2019.pdf (accessed 18 June 2020).

Ft.com. 2012. 'The End of Asia's Demographic Dividend'. *Financial Times* (online). Available at: https://www.ft.com/content/bd935806-6d00-11e1-a7c7-00144feab49a (accessed 5 January 2020).

Ghani, E. 2018. 'Demographic Dividend, Growth and Jobs'. *Livemint* (online). Available at: https://www.livemint.com/Opinion/Eo1PgYgUyKl9xgWLrLPwJP/Demographic-dividend-growth-and-jobs.html (accessed 1 June 2020).

The Global Goals. N.d. 'Goal 4: Quality Education' (online). Available at: https://www.globalgoals.org/4-quality-education (accessed 5 January 2020).

Jaffrelot, C., and Kalyankar, S. 2019. 'Demographic Dividend or Demographic Burden? India's Education Challenge'. Institut Montaigne (online). Available at: https://www.institutmontaigne.org/en/blog/demographic-dividend-or-demographic-burden-indias-education-challenge (accessed 1 June 2020).

McKinsey and Company. 2018. 'The Power of Parity: Advancing Women's Equality in Asia Pacific' (online). Available at: https://www.mckinsey.com/~/media/McKinsey/Featured%20Insights/Gender%20Equality/The%20power%20of%20parity%20Advancing%20womens%20equality%20in%20India%202018/India%20power%20of%20parity%20report.pdf (accessed 16 June 2020).

Mhrd.gov.in. 2019. 'School Education: Government of India, Ministry of Human Resource Development' (online). Available at: https://mhrd.gov.in/rte (accessed 7 January 2020).

National Crime Research Bureau (ncrb.gov.in). 2018. 'Crime in India 2018, Table 3A.2(i)', p. 7 (online). Available at: https://ncrb.gov.in/sites/default/files/crime_in_india_table_additional_table_chapter_reports/Table%203A.2_0.pdf.

Niti.gov.in. 2018. 'SDG India Index Baseline Report 2018', p. 54 (online). Available at: http://niti.gov.in/writereaddata/files/SDX_Index_India_21.12.2018.pdf (accessed 18 June 2020).

Ramya, M. 2012. 'Rote Learning an Evil in Education System, National Survey Reveals – Times of India' (online). *Times of India*. Available at: https://timesofindia.indiatimes.com/home/education/news/Rote-learning-an-evil-in-education-system-national-survey-reveals/articleshow/17564012.cms.

Safecity.in. (2015). 'Dwarka Campaign Casebook' (online). Available at: https://safecity.in/wp-content/uploads/2017/06/Dwarka-Campaign-Casebook.pdf.

———. 2017. 'Annual Report 2017–18' (online). Available at: http://safecity.in/wp-content/uploads/2019/01/RDF-Annual-Report-2018.pdf (accessed 16 June 2020).

———. N.d. 'Safecity' (online). Available at: http://www.safecity.in (accessed 5 January 2020).

Singh, D. 2018. 'Opinion: India's Demographic Dividend Will Play Out Over a Longer Span'. *Livemint* (online). Available at: https://www.livemint.com/Opinion/zgCdZ3GrDwtDpQWD95HenO/Opinion--Indias-demographic-dividend-will-play-out-over-a.html (accessed 1 June 2020).

Top Universities. N.d. 'Universities' (online). Available at: https://www.topuniversities.com/universities/country/india.

United Nations Population Fund (Unfpa.org). N.d. 'Demographic Dividend' (online). Available at: https://www.unfpa.org/demographic-dividend (accessed 1 June 2020).

Chapter 5

PUTTING THE AFRICAN GIRL AT THE CENTRE OF DEMOGRAPHIC CHANGE PROGRAMMES

Ekua Yankah

The African continent is on the verge of undergoing a historic transformation, ushering in a new age of opportunity. Demographic transition in sub-Saharan Africa is set to produce the largest workforce in history within the next 25 years (UNDP, 2016). The predictions for what this transition will mean for the African population are hopeful: 'If this period coincides with a broad-based and significant investment in human capital concentrated from youth to adulthood, along with opportunities in the labour market, the result is a boost in economic growth and prosperity for the population' (UNFPA, 2019).

However, the key to peace and prosperity rests on unlocking the untapped potential of the African girl child, who is the foundation for the success of African families and the future of the African continent. The main ingredient for the success of Africa is an educated and empowered woman in full control of realising her economic, social, sexual and reproductive rights.

> Without aggressive investment in girls aged 10 to 14, countries cannot count on reaping a demographic dividend [...] Not making these investments amounts to planned poverty.
>
> – Judith Bruce, Population Council, New York

Since the late 1990s, scholars have speculated about the factors that explain the relationship between population change and economic growth. Researchers agree that what is vital is the change in age structure of populations as women have fewer and safer births later in life (Bloom et al., 2000 and 2007; Bloom and Canning, 2004),[1] in addition to the characteristics and opportunities of

---

1 'Fertility has declined rapidly in a few countries with unfavorable development conditions (e.g., Bangladesh, Indonesia, Nepal, and Sri Lanka). These are traditional,

the population, especially around education (Lutz et al., 2008), health and employment (Joshi and Schultz, 2007). Experience shows that supportive investments in the human capital of young people need to be made over time. Early phase investments facilitate the dividend whereas later investments maintain the dividend. The decisive factor is that the demographic dividend is directly linked to gender policies. This is common sense when one considers that working populations increase when women can productively enter the labour market (UNFPA, 2019). As the economic status of African women and girls improves, it has a ripple effect for entire families, communities and countries (UNDP, 2016).

Gender Gap and Steps Forward

Gender equality for women and girls is far from being achieved. Great gains have been made in achieving universal primary education. By 2014, reportedly all African countries had achieved parity in primary school education (UNECA, 2015). However, big gaps remain in addressing parity in secondary school education. Gender inequality is still prevalent in secondary and tertiary education. In West Africa, for example, the gender gap for secondary school education is almost 50 per cent (World Bank, 2014). The number of out-of-school children is unacceptably high, and girls disproportionately account for 56 per cent of all out-of-school children (UNESCO, 2014).

In terms of health, women and girls face continued challenges in the African region due to factors such as early marriage, sexual and physical violence, maternal mortality and HIV and AIDS. Notable successes were achieved in the 15 years leading up to the Millennium Development Goals (MDGs) due to heavy investments in human capital development. By 2015, maternal mortality had declined by 45 per cent in sub-Saharan Africa and by 59 per cent in North Africa. Despite progress, much work remains to be done in this area. In 2015, the African continent registered 546 maternal deaths per 100,000 births compared to a world average of 215 deaths per 100,000 births and 12 deaths per 100,000 births in industrialised countries (WHO, 2015). Uneducated and poor women and girls living in rural and remote areas of the continent are most at risk. The high proportion of girls giving birth under the age of 18 years

---

poor, rural, and agricultural societies, yet fertility has declined to low levels. The main explanation for this unexpected trend is the priority their governments have given to social development (e.g., schooling and women's empowerment) and the implementation of effective family planning and health programs. No fertility decline has been observed in a poor and largely illiterate country in the absence of a strong family planning program' (Bongaarts et al., 2012).

poses a threat to maternal health due to the risk of complications for mother and baby. HIV infection remains an area of great concern. In Eastern and Southern Africa, young women under the age of 24 years account for more than three-quarters of all newly acquired HIV infections (UNAIDS, 2019).

African women account for a large share of the workforce with almost 7 out of 10 women engaging in some form of formal or informal labour. The share is larger compared to other regions of the world with 6 out of 10 women in North America and only 5 out of 10 women in Europe, Asia and the Pacific. However, the majority of African women and girls work in low-paid and low-productive work in the non-formal sector lacking opportunities for career advancement or job protection.

Compared to men, African women continue to suffer from significant gender disparities in the labour market. These disparities are found in women's access to economic assets (i.e. loans), workplace participation, entrepreneurship opportunities and use of natural resources. A gender wage gap of about 30 per cent is prevalent across all labour markets. On top of that, African women and girls perform the lion's share of care and domestic work, including child and elderly care, cooking, cleaning and fetching water. Economies lag when women are not fully integrated in labour markets. Figures show that gender inequality in the labour market cost sub-Saharan Africa about US$95 billion annually between 2010 and 2014, peaking at US$105 billion in 2014. These results confirm that without educated women, African labour markets are not living up to their full growth potential (UNDP, 2016).

In terms of civic engagement, women's representation at the highest levels of politics has become a reality on the African continent. Since 1995, there have been four female heads of state in Liberia, Malawi, the Central African Republic and Mauritius. In 2012, Her Excellency Dr. Nkosazana Dlamini Zuma became the first female chairperson to head the African Union Commission. Rwanda is the global leader with 64 per cent female representation in the houses of parliament closely followed by the Seychelles, Senegal and South Africa. Women are also strongly represented in regional and local political organisations. The fact that ever more African women are engaged in politics is helping to overcome deeply entrenched inequalities in postcolonial political systems (UNDP, 2016).

The Human Rights Approach to Development

For the past 75 years, the international community, together with regional bodies, has put in place a wide array of legal norms, precedents and legislation to lift the profile of women's rights. This section of the chapter will provide an overview of landmark human rights frameworks that revolutionised girl- and women-centred development (see Table 5.1). The 1979 Convention on the Elimination of All Forms of Discrimination Against Women (CEDAW) is also known as the International Bill of Rights for Women stating that women and girls have the right to live free of discrimination. A total of 189 countries worldwide ratified CEDAW.

Some four years later, at the UN World Conference on Human Rights in Vienna, delegates lobbied for the statement that the rights of women and of the girl-child are an inalienable, integral and indivisible part of universal human rights. It is important to mention that the ratification of the Convention of the Rights of the Child (1990) played an important role in this context as it affirmed the rights of girls under the age of 18. These three events were unprecedented because the advancement of women and girls became firmly entrenched in international law.

> The human rights of women and of the girl-child are an inalienable, integral and indivisible part of universal human rights. The full and equal participation of women in political, civil, economic, social and cultural life, at the national, regional and international levels, and the eradication of all forms of discrimination on grounds of sex are priority objectives of the international community. Gender-based violence and all forms of sexual harassment and exploitation, including those resulting from cultural prejudice and international trafficking, are incompatible with the dignity and worth of the human person, and must be eliminated. (UN General Assembly, 1993, Article 18)

The true watershed moment, however, was the International Conference on Population and Development (ICPD) in Cairo in 1994. The ICPD Programme of Action set forth a new paradigm for responding to population growth by stating that fulfilling the rights of girls and women was central to addressing development. The ICPD Programme of Action asserted that the empowerment and autonomy of women and the improvement of their political, social, economic and health status was highly important as an end in itself as well as for achieving sustainable development (UNFPA, 2019). ICPD outlined the essential links between sexual and reproductive health and rights with almost every other aspect of development: urbanisation, migration, ageing, changing family structures and the rights of young people (UNFPA, 2019).

What the Cairo conference did is to say that in order to lift the developmental status of countries, we need to improve the holistic well-being of women and girls because it is their inalienable right to live a good life. ICPD put a firm end to an era of population control, focused on restricting women's reproductive capacity focusing instead on sexual, reproductive and health rights. Finally, the Fourth United Nations Conference on Women held in

Table 5.1 Summary of human rights frameworks specifying the rights of women and girls

Convention on the Elimination of Discrimination against Women (1979, New York)	**Convention on the Rights of the Child (1990, New York)**	**United Nations World Conference on Human Rights (1993, Vienna)**	**International Conference on Population and Development (1994, Cairo)**	**Fourth World Conference on Women (1995, Beijing)**
The International Bill of Rights for Women: defines the right of women to be free from discrimination CEDAW is the only human rights treaty that affirms the reproductive rights of women	Sets out the civil, political, economic, social, health and cultural rights of children with the guiding principles of: non-discrimination; adherence to the best interests of the child; the right to life, survival and development; and the right to participate	The human rights of women and of the girl child are an inalienable, integral and indivisible part of universal human rights	Asserted that the empowerment and autonomy of women and the improvement of their political, social, economic and health status was highly important end in itself as well as for achieving sustainable development	The Beijing Declaration and Platform for Action is an agenda for women's empowerment and considered the key global policy document on gender equality

Source: UNFPA and UN Women.

Beijing in 1995 generated commitments to advance a wider range of women's rights such as targets for women's representation in politics.

At the regional level, the African Union has complemented international frameworks with its own legal structures, taking into account African priorities. There are three regional instruments that promote gender equality and human rights for women and girls: the African Charter on Human and Peoples' Rights, the Protocol to the African Charter on Human and Peoples' Rights on the Rights of Women in Africa (the 'Maputo Protocol') and the Solemn Declaration on Gender Equality in Africa (the Solemn Declaration, or SDGEA) (UNDP, 2016).

UNFPA+50, ICPD+25 and Beijing+25

As the world celebrates several historic anniversaries in 2020, that is, the United Nation Population Fund's 50th anniversary, UN Women's 10th anniversary, ICPD+25 and Beijing+25, the international community will look forward and back to assess progress in supporting demographic change on the African continent (Lancet Editorial, 2020). What are some of the common threads in countries that have successfully managed demographic change? UNFPA has named its flagship State of the World's Population 2019 'Unfinished Business'. In its opening pages, the authors state, 'The pursuits of rights and choice is an ongoing one, with new challenges appearing all the time' (UNFPA, 2019). Despite progress made, hundreds of millions of women and girls face economic, social, cultural and institutional barriers that prevent them from realising their sexual and reproductive rights and goals (UNFPA, 2019). On the continent, in particular, this is fuelled by the presence of harmful social norms in the form of conservative religious beliefs, tribal identity, job and educational discrimination, sexual violence, early marriage, social stigma, harmful traditional practices such as female genital cutting and other gender-based practices that limit opportunities for women and girls (UNDP, 2016). Yet harmful social norms also affect men and boys and communities as a whole, preventing everyone from achieving their highest human potential.

In November 2019, the Nairobi Summit on ICPD+25 ended with bold commitments by world leaders to end all maternal deaths, address the unmet need for family planning and also address gender-based violence (e.g. rape as a weapon of war) and practices harmful to women and girls in the next decade (Nairobi Summit, 2019). The governments of Kenya and Denmark, the summit's hosts, want ICPD+25 to be remembered as the moment that set in motion concrete actions to save millions of mothers from mortality, lift women and girls from exclusion and marginalisation and enable countries to harness the demographic dividend (Nairobi Summit, 2019).

Successful Girl-Centred Programming on the Ground: Case study – The Population Council's Programmes in Ethiopia

In Ethiopia, the Population Council partners with government agencies, including the Federal Ministry of Women, Children and Youth Affairs, local faith-based and non-governmental organisations and international NGOs such as the YWCA and Handicap International. Biruh Tesfa (Bright future), Berhane Hewan (Light for Eve) and Meseret Hiwot (Base of life) are three programmes it has successfully run for adolescent girls and young women aged 10–24 (Popcouncil.org, 2020).

Biruh Tesfa started in 2006 and invited the poorest adolescent girls and young women (7–24 years) in rural areas to join female mentor–led 'safe spaces' that were linked to health services; here they would receive training in literacy and numeracy, life skills, financial literacy and entrepreneurship. The unique feature of Biruh Tesfa is that participants were recruited by going from door-to-door to reach out to the most vulnerable girls, such as child domestic workers, children with disabilities and child sex workers. The programme reached more than 75,000 out-of-school girls in 18 cities in Ethiopia, including the capital, Addis Ababa (Popcouncil.org, 2020).

An impact evaluation of the programme found that among girls who had never received formal schooling, participation in Biruh Tesfa significantly increased mean test scores in reading and numeracy. Programme participants were also twice as likely to report having social support, scoring well on HIV knowledge questions and knowing where to get voluntary counselling and testing. Building on its previous success, Biruh Tesfa is being scaled up to reach 10,500 more adolescent girls in forced domestic work and those with visual, hearing, mobility and intellectual impairments (Popcouncil.org, 2020). Programme Directory Haney Shamil says: 'Biruh Tesfa has already proven effective not only at reaching vulnerable girls, but improving their lives'.[2]

When girls are married as children, it sets them off on a path of isolation, disadvantage and hardship. In response to the high prevalence of child marriage in three African countries, the Population Council developed Berhane Hewan, an award-winning, rigorously evaluated programme aiming to increase the age at marriage among adolescent girls in Ethiopia, Tanzania and Burkina Faso. The programme uses a holistic approach engaging adolescent girls, their families and their communities. By initiating innovative 'community conversations', communities were encouraged to discuss the consequences of child marriage. Families of adolescent girls received school

---

2 https://www.popcouncil.org/news/biruh-tesfa-to-scale-up-targeting-pivotal-population-of-vulnerable-girls-in.

supplies or uniforms in order to reduce the economic barriers of sending girls to school. Furthermore, families who kept girls unmarried during the two-year programme period were awarded a chicken for each year (Popcouncil.org, 2015).

Evaluation results in Ethiopia showed that all three intervention components (education support, receiving a chicken for staying unmarried, community conversations) and all components combined delayed marriage significantly. In communities where girls aged between 12 and 14 were offered educational support, nearly all (94 per cent) were less likely to be married at the end of the study. In Tanzania, all intervention components were combined, with girls aged 15–17 years receiving a goat for every year they remained unmarried and in school. The study also showed significant reductions in child marriages. The Berhane Hewan study in Burkina Faso is still ongoing. Results are expected soon (Popcouncil.org, 2015).

Mesert Hiwott is a mentor-led education programme targeting married girls in rural parts of Ethiopia, with HIV prevention and providing reproductive health services being its goals. Replicating the methodology developed for Biruh Tesfa, trained adult female mentors go door-to-door to recruit eligible adolescent girls and young women aged 10–24 to attend education sessions in community-run 'safe spaces' (Popcouncil.org, 2013).

Programmatic Lessons Learned

This section will review the guiding principles of girl-centred programming in development and lists a set of recommendations for successful programming in the African context. It will also suggest roles donor countries could play in guiding countries looking for support.

Sustainable change is only possible in a context where governments have committed to leadership and accountability for women and girls. The main ingredient for the success of the African continent is an educated and empowered African woman in full control of realising her economic, social, cultural, sexual and reproductive rights. In order to achieve this goal, countries could be helped to make broad-based and significant investments in human capital.

1. In the education sector, renewed investments should address gender parity in secondary and tertiary education to reduce the considerable number of out-of-school girls across the continent. Evidence from various countries has shown the benefit of employing conditional and unconditional cash transfers to support the most disadvantaged households with the costs of sending their daughters to school (Akresh et al., 2013; Baird

et al., 2015; Chaudhury and Parajuli, 2006). This is complemented with continued investments in building up a cadre of trained teachers, school infrastructures and strategies to improve the quality of education.

2. Donor-funded, community-led programmes such as DREAMS and Biruh Tesfa have shown the benefit of reaching out to the most marginalised women and girls in rural areas and peri-urban slums, including married and out-of-school girls and young women, with evidence-based content for non-formal education, HIV prevention, entrepreneurship training and a voucher system for accessing essential health services and post-rape care. New evidence suggests that complementary programmes must also reach out to boys and young men.
3. In the area of health, increasing the legal age of marriage and enforcing a ban on all forms of child marriage and other harmful practices will have a significant impact on reducing the rates of adolescent pregnancy and maternal and infant mortality and halt the cycle of intergenerational poverty, exclusion and disadvantage. Programmes employing holistic approaches that target girls from a young age, as early as 7, and include parents, community members and religious leaders have shown promising results in Ethiopia, Tanzania and Burkina Faso. Other community-wide programmes such as SASA! and Stepping Stones[3] have proven effective in reducing incidents of gender-based violence in communities.
4. Reducing maternal mortality to zero cannot be achieved without addressing the hot topic of abortion, reforming abortion laws, making post-abortion care widely available and addressing the legal age of consent for girls to access services. This is especially urgent in fragile states where the rape of women and girls is used as a weapon of war. This must be complemented with work to address the unmet need for contraception, women and girls' access to services, including shelters and safe spaces, and community-wide access to comprehensive sexuality education for children, adolescents and adults of all ages.
5. Structured efforts to address gender inequality in labour markets include women and girl's favoured access to economic assets, entrepreneurship opportunities, participation and advancement in the formal job market and other forms of economic security such as ownership and inheritance of land rights.

3 SASA! is a groundbreaking community mobilisation approach developed by the Ugandan NGO Raising Voice for preventing violence against women and HIV. Stepping Stones is a social norms training package addressing gender, HIV, communication and relationship skills originally developed in rural Uganda.

6. Finally, addressing the issue of violence and violence as a method of war is an integral aspect of protecting women and girls in war and conflict as well as in the home. All governments have a great interest in ensuring peace and security for the entire population. International donor support is needed to aid women and children living in fragile states to be free from violence and realise their human rights.

References

Akresh, R., De Walque, D., and Kazianga, H. 2013. 'Cash Transfers and Child Schooling – Evidence from a Randomized Evaluation of the Role of Conditionality'. World Bank Policy Research Working Paper no. 6340. Washington, DC: World Bank.

Baird, S., Chirwa, E., McIntosh, C., and Özler, B. 2015. 'What Happens Once the Intervention Ends? The Medium-Term Impacts of a Cash Transfer Programme in Malawi'. 3ie Impact Evaluation Report 27. New Delhi: International Initiative for Impact Evaluation (3ie).

Bloom, D. E., and Canning, D. 2004. 'Global Demographic Change: Dimensions and Economic Significance'. Proceedings: Economic Policy Symposium, Jackson Hole, Federal Reserve Bank of Kansas City, August: 9–56.

Bloom, D. E., Bloom, D. E., Canning, D., and Malaney, P. N. 2000. 'Population Dynamics and Economic Growth in Asia'. *Population and Development Review: Population and Economic Change in East Asia* Supplement 26: 257–90.

———. 2007. 'Fertility, Female Labor Force Participation, and the Demographic Dividend'. Working Paper no. 25. Cambridge, MA: Harvard School of Public Health Program on the Global Demography of Aging.

Bongaarts. J., Cleland, J., Townsend, J. W., Bertrand, J. T., and Das Gupta, M. 2012. *Family Planning Programs for the 21st Century: Rationale and Design.* New York: Population Council.

Chaudhury, N., and Parajuli, D. 2006. 'Conditional Cash Transfers and Female Schooling: The Impact of the Female School Stipend Program on Public School Enrollments in Punjab, Pakistan'. World Bank Policy Research Paper no. 4102. Washington, DC: World Bank.

Joshi, S., and Schultz, T. 2007. 'Family Planning as an Investment in Development: Evaluation of a Program's Consequences in Matlab, Bangladesh' (online). Econpapers.repec.org. Available at: https://econpapers.repec.org/paper/izaizadps/dp2639.htm (accessed 24 March 2020).

Lancet Editorial. 2020. '2020: A Critical Year for Women, Gender Equity, and Health'. *Lancet* 395(10217): P1.

Lutz, W., Lutz, W., Cuaresma, J. C. and Sandersen, W. 2008. 'The Demography of Educational Attainment and Economic Growth'. *Science* 319(5866): 1047–48.

Nairobi Summit. 2019. 'Nairobi Summit on ICPD25 Ends with a Clear Path Forward to Transform the World for Women and Girls' (online). Available at: https://www.nairobisummiticpd.org/news/nairobi-summit-icpd25-ends-clear-path-forward-transform-world-women-and-girls (accessed 15 December 2019).

Popcouncil.org. 2013. 'Meseret Hiwott ("Base of Life") | Population Council' (online). Available at: https://www.popcouncil.org/research/meseret-hiwott-base-of-life (accessed 15 December 2019).

———. 2015. 'Building an Evidence Base to Delay Marriage in Sub-Saharan Africa | Population Council' (online). Available at: https://www.popcouncil.org/research/building-an-evidence-base-to-delay-marriage-in-sub-saharan-africa (accessed 15 December 2019).

———. 2020. 'Biruh Tesfa ("Bright Future") | Population Council' (online). Available at: https://www.popcouncil.org/research/biruh-tesfa-safe-spaces-for-out-of-school-girls-in-urban-slum-areas-of-ethi (accessed 24 March 2020).

UN General Assembly. 1993. 'Vienna Declaration and Programme of Action'. World Conference on Human Rights, Vienna, 14–25 June, A/CONF. 157/23.

UNAIDS. 2019. *Women and HIV: A Spotlight on Adolescent Girls and Young Women.* Geneva: UNAIDS.

UNDP. 2016. *Africa Human Development Report 2016: Accelerating Gender Equality and Women's Empowerment in Africa.* New York: UNDP.

UNECA. 2015. *Assessing Progress in Africa toward the Millennium Development Goals: 2015 MDG Report – Lessons Learned in Implementing the MDGs.* Addis Ababa: UNECA.

UNESCO. 2014. 'Progress in Getting All Children to School Stalls but Some Countries Show the Way Forward'. Policy Paper 14/Fact Sheet 28. Paris: UNESCO.

UNFPA. 2019. 'Unfinished Business – The Pursuit of Rights and Choices for All' (online). Available at: https://youtu.be/7UD7QXJ_Yy4 (accessed 12 December 2019).

———. n.d. 'The Human Rights of Women' (online). Available at: https://www.unfpa.org/resources/human-rights-women (accessed 11 December 2019).

WHO. 2015. 'Trends in Maternal Mortality: 1990 to 2015'. Geneva: WHO. http://apps.who.int/iris/bitstream/10665/194254/1/9789241565141_eng.pdf?ua=1 (accessed 15 December 2019).

World Bank. 2014. *Gender at Work: A Companion to the World Development Report on Jobs.* Washington, DC.

Chapter 6

FROM INCARCERATION TO TRANSFORMATION: EX-GANG MEMBERS AS ACTORS OF CHANGE IN LOS ANGELES

Sonja Peteranderl

They called her 'Sweetie' in the gang. At the age of 11, her brothers would have her sit in front of a doughnut shop and squeeze out tears. She told people she had lost her dog. When someone offered to help her, she led them to a street nearby – where her brothers mugged the helpers. 'It's not a nice name, it was basically made from manipulating folks', Linda Gomez says. 'I have remorse, regret for the people I hurt along the way. But that's also part of who I am. That's why I am in this fight today.'

Gomez, a 37-year-old former gang member living in South Los Angeles, has spent a considerable part of her life behind prison walls. Nowadays, she uses her experience to transform her community for the better and support others to carve out a future for themselves.

At the age of 11, Gomez was already a member of the gang HMT 13 and part of her siblings' drug peddling family business: 'My oldest brother started cooking speed at his home in the kitchen, so me and my other brother sold it', she recounts. As a minor, she could get away with offenses, so she stored drugs and stole food from stores to fill their fridge. Despite their drug sales, the siblings constantly ran out of money due to the addiction of the oldest brother: 'It was a revolving door. All the money we made he put in his nose, so we had to keep trying to make more money. Also when we got our money we wanted to floss (*show off*), show love to our homies, throw big parties or whatever.'

Divided Cities

The involvement of minors in the illegal drug trade and other illicit businesses of gangs and cartels is a growing concern worldwide (Breckin, 2019; Dodd,

2019; Dowdney, 2003; Porio and Crisol, 2004). Like many young people of colour from neglected neighbourhoods, Linda Gomez had limited options to choose from. Los Angeles is a divided city, a 'combination of regulation, discrimination, structural inequality, and violence' has led to a racially and economically fragmented city (Gibbons, 2018, p. 1). More than half of the black families in LA live in the poorest quarter of neighbourhoods in consecutive generations, compared to only 7 per cent of white families (p. 2). In one of America's main hubs for immigrants, even highly skilled immigrants struggle to find jobs and are often forced to take on rudimentary jobs or end up unemployed, leading to a massive 'brain waste' (Batalova et al., 2016). The United States 'performs poorly in two areas where its superiority is usually simply taken for granted: incorporating traditionally disadvantaged groups into the paid labour force and providing opportunities for economic mobility' (Schmitt and Zipperer, 2006, p. 1).

Finding solutions for this waste of human talent is crucial: The United States is currently challenged by a demographic decline with 'masses of workers reaching retirement age, and smaller generations replacing them', causing a dampening effect on the economy (Irwin, 2019). While the United States is struggling with an aging population, the country fails to provide a large share of its youth, especially from low-income communities, with the resources they would need to succeed in society and become active contributors to society and economy rather than a burden – depriving itself of a valuable, yet shrinking resource.

Growing into the Gang

Linda Gomez's mother lost her job as a nurse as she was suffering from epilepsy seizures. Linda grew up in a low-income housing unit in Hemet, Riverside County, east of LA (Figure 6.1). 'There were a lot of drugs there, a lot of gangs. I was happy, because there was always a bunch of kids to play with', she describes her childhood. 'But our idea of playing was different. We would go break windows, start fires right on walls. We sat in the back of the apartments huffing inhalants. I smoked my first cigarette when I was 7 and when I was 9, I smoked my first joint. It was normal.'

Gangs were part of the community. When her brothers started hanging out with members of the local street gang HMT 13, she played with their younger siblings. 'We were the next generation of gang-bangers', she says. 'When I was 11, I and all my buddys got jumped into the same gang.' They had to prove their courage in an initiation ritual in which the newcomers had to fight against several established members. 'When I got jumped in, I felt like I was accepted by them', Gomez explains. 'I don't think there's anybody that

Figure 6.1 At the age of 11, Linda Gomez became a member of the street gang HMT 13, and at 17, she was sentenced to almost 25 years in prison. Today, she is committed to helping her community build a better future. Credit: Sonja Peteranderl.

turns to a gang who doesn't have co-dependency issues or self-esteem issues. You want that acceptance so bad.' Her brothers and sister used to beat her up frequently, as revenge for what they had suffered at the hands of their father. He had made the youngest daughter, Linda, watch, while he hit, humiliated, tortured the other children – so 'everything that he did to them, they did to me. They broke my nose three times, broke my wrists, the last thing they broke was my toe. That was a reason why it was so important for me to be accepted by the gang.'

Gangs as Social Organisations

Even gangs like the infamous Mara Salvatrucha (MS-13) could be regarded as 'a social organisation first, and a criminal organisation second', according to researchers from InSight Crime and American University's Center for Latin American & Latino Studies (CLALS). 'The gang is not about generating revenue as much as it is about creating a collective identity that is constructed and reinforced by shared, often criminal experiences, especially acts of violence and expressions of social control' (2018, p. 3). It could also be understood as 'a byproduct of war, migration and policy' (p. 6) or a 'dangerous but predictable response to abuse and social marginalization' (p. 9). Central American refugees in the United States who had fled the civil war faced limited economic opportunities, discrimination and threats by local gangs in the United States in the 1970s. Over the next decade, formerly non-violent Salvadoran youth groups radicalised: 'Knives, machetes and even axes soon replaced fists. Territory became more important to the gang's identity than music or drugs. And they expanded' (p. 14) – and the MS-13 transformed into a violent street gang with 50,000 and 70,000 members in Central America and countries with a larger Central American diaspora, respectively (p. 14). Law enforcement efforts in the United States and large-scale deportations of gang members in the 1990s also exported the phenomenon to the Northern Triangle countries of El Salvador, Guatemala and Honduras where prison and street gangs (maras) threaten the state, businesses and citizens today, but also bribe or collaborate with corrupt security forces and politicians (p. 15).

'Because of the structural character of the gang in contemporary societies, they are disproportionately composed of people from low-income backgrounds who want what everyone else wants in the USA and are prepared to get it by whatever means necessary', Sanchez-Jankowski argues (2003, p. 192). International case studies prove that family income inequalities and child poverty elevate subsequent risks for self-harm and violent criminality (Mok et al., 2018). On the other hand, explanations why youth end up in gangs should not be oversimplified: The majority of youth who struggle with identity problems and/or come from broken and poor homes do not end up in gangs (Sanchez-Jankowski, 2003, p. 193).

The School-to-Prison Pipeline

However, structural inequalities contribute to a disproportionate tendency among people of colour to become incarcerated, a phenomenon debated in the United States as the 'school-to-prison pipeline' (Lind and Nelson, 2015): black and brown children are more prone to experience negative outcomes in school, are more frequently controlled by police compared to white children and have a disproportionately higher probability of becoming involved in the juvenile justice system.

In Los Angeles (Figure 6.2), the Rodney King scandal and the riots of 1992 became the symbol of the broken relationship between law enforcement and communities, but studies and statistics prove structural racial bias, over-policing and a higher risk of police violence for black and brown

Figure 6.2 Torn city: Areas like South Los Angeles struggle with structural disadvantage, poverty and gang violence. Credit: Sonja Peteranderl.

youth and adults have been stable until today. 'The existence of disproportionate racial representation in the juvenile justice system raises questions about fundamental fairness and equality of treatment of these youth by the police, courts, and other personnel connected with the juvenile justice system' (McCord et al., 2001, p. 228). If children are criminalised from childhood on, even before they commit their first crimes, there is a severe impact on their prospects.

Linda Gomez grew up in the 1990s era, when the controversial 'Zero Tolerance' policy was introduced and even schools started to punish minor offences with suspensions, expulsions and arrests (American Psychologist, 2008). US schools have since become heavily policed places, with their own police units and increasing technological surveillance (Beckett, 2019). Advocates criticise a lack of oversight and regulations and demand alternative programmes that rather focus on the behaviour of students instead of punishment. In the 2016–17 school year, the Los Angeles Unified School District (LAUSD) directed US$67.34 million of its US$13.5 billion budget to school police – while restorative justice programmes received just US$10.81 million (Hennessy, 2017).

Suspects once registered by law enforcement become part of a surveillance and arrest cycle: suspects of gang membership are included in gang databases, but the criteria are unclear; errors frequently occur (Clayton, 2019; Miller, 2020). California had to overhaul its CalGang database after an audit revealed a lack of oversight in 2016 and severe errors. People were incorrectly labelled as gang members, and even children as young as 2 years old had entries (California State Auditor, 2016).

School became a turning point for Linda Gomez when the administration called the police on her. She was sent to juvenile hall at the age of 11 for the possession and sales of methamphetamine to other children at school. 'I wasn't really out on the streets after the age of 11; no more than three months. I was either in a social programme or in a juvenile hall', she says. She quickly climbed the criminal ladder, from selling drugs and burglary to stealing cars and selling them. Being a gang member, a serial offender, became part of her identity: 'I accepted it, I embraced it. When you're growing up in that environment you become institutionalised.' She believed that she belonged on the inside of the criminal world, of a cell, unlike 'normal' people. 'The free world people' is how she called them.

Turnaround in Prison

When Linda Gomez was 17, a night in one of the gang's kickback houses turned violent. Together with other teen girls, she beat up and tortured a girl who allegedly betrayed her boyfriend. They tattooed her on the face and her hand and held her in the gang hideout for one and a half days. They were charged with aggravated mayhem and false imprisonment. For Linda, her gang membership was the most severely valued aspect. Alleged gang ties can lead to longer prison sentences and might be considered more serious than the offense itself, which is subject of a controversial debate (Clayton, 2019). Back then, California's Proposition 21 policy had just gone into effect trying minors as adults and adding extra prison time for gang-related crimes: Linda was sentenced to 24 years and 8 months in prison. 'We were the poster children for the new proposition', she says. She stresses that she doesn't want to justify the violent acts she committed: 'I think it was one of my snapping points. I just took out everything I felt for my dad, for my brothers and sister, teachers on this girl I didn't even know.'

Prison became a turning point. At first, the cell reminded her of the closets her brothers had locked her in – locked in a box, lights out, scared. But she adapted quickly, continuing her criminal lifestyle behind prison walls: 'You just get into survival mode.' In 2010, she was asked to join a programme which facilitated an exchange between inmates and youth. After she had told the students how she ended up in prison, a girl asked her questions she had never asked herself before: How had she felt as a little girl? Did she have anger towards her dad? Linda Gomez found out that the girl later reported that her dad had molested and beat her. She did not want to suppress the anger like Linda Gomez had, potentially leading her onto a similar path. 'The feeling that the girl had given me was like I finally did something good for somebody. I never felt like that before, no drugs ever made me feel like that', Gomez says. 'I reflected on my life, looking at the choices I made. That was the first time I realised I'm actually in prison.' In the programme 'Bridges to Life', she dealt with restorative justice and drew on her lifeline to understand her experiences, to reveal patterns and feelings.

Actors of Change

Still incarcerated, Gomez co-founded 'Generation to Generation', a self-help group for gang members who wanted to adapt to a new mindset, change their behaviour – and learn from people who know how gang mentality works first-hand: 'If I understand and reach you, I can teach you stuff I have learned like no other', Gomez says. 'Also I can talk about things they can relate to: about cooking meth and staying up at night because you got to sell more drugs so you could put some fucking food in the fridge or you go the bathroom trying to flush the toilet and the water's gone.'

In 2014, a new law, the Senate Bill (SB) 260 offered youth offender parole hearings for prisoners like Gomez who were under the age of 18 at the time of their crimes (Prison Law Office, 2016). She was finally released on parole in 2018 – 8 years earlier than expected – and the LA-based gang intervention programme Homeboy Industries offered her a place in their 18-month-long trainee programme for former gang members.

More than 600,000 formerly incarcerated people return to their communities every year without the support to successfully transition back to their homes, struggling to find jobs – and thus being at risk to return to their criminal lifestyle. 'For those who are black or hispanic – especially women – the status as "formerly incarcerated" reduces their employment chances even more. This perpetual labour market punishment creates a counterproductive system of release and poverty, hurting everyone involved: employers, the taxpayers, and certainly formerly incarcerated people looking to break the cycle' (Couloute and Kopf, 2018). But success stories and role models like Gomez prove that it is key to perceive former inmates or gang members as a resource, rather than a risk. They can become actors of change if they are provided with support and opportunities – not just contributing to the transformation of their communities, but also of the justice system and societies at large with their insider perspectives.

Gomez is currently working as a civic engagement specialist at Community Coalition, an NGO with the mission to 'transform the social and economic conditions in South LA that foster addiction, crime, violence and poverty by building a community institution that involves thousands in creating, influencing and changing public policy' (Community Coalition, 2020). The organisation was founded in 1990 as a response to the crack cocaine epidemic and the brutal law enforcement tactics and laws. It wanted to develop alternative, grassroots solutions to the public health crisis and the social injustice. Current initiatives involve mapping liquor stores in the area as well as unused lots to force the stores to close down and turn empty spaces into public parks.

Linda Gomez realised how inequality shaped her biography: 'Some of this stuff was already a little shaped for us to make our choices. It's not by chance that right next to our apartment was a liquor store. It's not to make an excuse for what happened, it's just calling the system out for what it is.' Today, she tries to change this system with her work. She educates community members, goes from door to door or talks to people on the phone and encourages them to spread the word about initiatives. 'I never knew this was possible because I thought things like gangs are just your circle, but you need to get your circle educated, push them out, bring them in line.' Gomez also wants to ensure that her bad experiences with the public education system and overcrowded, underfunded classrooms will not continue in the future. She engages in the 'Schools & Communities First' campaign (2020) that advocates for closing commercial property tax loopholes for corporations and investors in California – allowing it to redirect US$12 billion tax money to California's schools and communities every year.

The criminal-turned-activist has become a role model for the next generation of local leaders who are trained at Community Coalition. Workshops and fellowship programmes provide them with tools to develop projects, lobby for change and become decision-makers in the political landscape of Los Angeles. Linda Gomez is dreaming of setting up her own social organisation for youth at risk in the future. 'I really got into self-help and the power of it', she says. 'I had thought that moving gangs and moving drugs was power, but helping people is just so different – and you can move so many people with community organising, but in a positive way.'

References

American Psychologist. 2008. 'Are Zero Tolerance Policies Effective in the Schools? An Evidentiary Review and Recommendations'. 63(9), 852–62.

Batalova, J., Fix, M., and Bachmeier, J. 2016. 'The Costs of Brain Waste among Highly Skilled Immigrants in the United States' (online). Available at: https://www.migrationpolicy.org/research/untapped-talent-costs-brain-waste-among-highly-skilled-immigrants-united-states#overlay-context=research/costs-brain-waste-among-highly-skilled-immigrants-united-states (accessed 15 January 2020).

Bates, K., and Sastry, A. 2017. 'When LA Erupted in Anger' (online). Available at: https://www.npr.org/2017/04/26/524744989/when-la-erupted-in-anger-a-look-back-at-the-rodney-king-riots?t=1578551907440 (accessed 11 March 2020).

Beckett, L. 2019. 'Under Digital Surveillance: How American Schools Spy on Millions of Kids'. *Guardian* (online). Available at: https://www.theguardian.com/world/2019/oct/22/school-student-surveillance-bark-gaggle (accessed 15 February 2020).

Breckin, E. 2019. 'Los Halcones: The Forgotten Children in Mexico's Organized Crime Conflict'. *Children, Youth and Environments*, 29(2), 119.

California State Auditor. 2016. 'The CalGang Criminal Intelligence System' (online). Available at: https://www.auditor.ca.gov/pdfs/reports/2015–130.pdf (accessed 5 January 2020).

Clayton, A. 2019. '92% Black or Latino: The California Laws That Keep Minorities in Prison. *Guardian* (online). Available at: https://www.theguardian.com/us-news/2019/nov/26/california-gang-enhancements-laws-black-latinos (accessed 11 December 2019).

Community Coalition. 2020. 'Our Story – Community Coalition' (online). Available at: http://cocosouthla.org/our-story/ (accessed 10 March 2020).

Couloute, L., and Kopf, D. 2018. 'Out of Prison & Out of Work' (online). Prisonpolicy.org. Available at: https://www.prisonpolicy.org/reports/outofwork.html (accessed 12 March 2020).

Dodd, V. 2019. 'Children as Young as Seven "Being Enslaved by UK Drug Gangs" '. *Guardian* (online). Available at: https://www.theguardian.com/society/2019/jul/05/children-as-young-as-seven-being-enslaved-by-uk-drug-gangs (accessed 11 March 2020).

Dowdney, L. 2003. *Children of the Drug Trade*. Rio de Janeiro: 7 Letras.

Gibbons, A. 2018. *City of Segregation: One Hundred Years of Struggle for Housing in Los Angeles*. 1st ed. London: Verso.

Hennessy, K. 2017. 'Counselors, Not Cops: Advocates Urge LAUSD to Increase Restorative Justice Funding' (online). Available at: https://chronicleofsocialchange.org/news-2/counselors-not-cops-advocates-urge-lausd-increase-restorative-justice-funding/26955 (accessed 4 January 2020).

InSight Crime and American University's Center for Latin American & Latino Studies (CLALS). 2018. 'MS-13 in the Americas. How the World's Most Notorious Gang Defies Logic, Resists Destruction' (online). Available at: https://www.insightcrime.org/wp-content/uploads/2018/02/MS13-in-the-Americas-InSight-Crime-English.pdf (accessed 10 January 2020).

Irwin, N. 2019. 'America's Biggest Economic Challenge May Be Demographic Decline' (online). Available at: https://www.nytimes.com/2019/04/03/upshot/americas-biggest-economic-challenge-may-be-demographic-decline.html (accessed 4 January 2020).

Lind, D., and Nelson, L. 2015. 'The School to Prison Pipeline, Explained – Justice Policy Institute' (online). Available at: http://www.justicepolicy.org/news/8775 (accessed 10 March 2020).

Los Angeles Times. 2020. ' "Stop-and-Frisk in a Car": Elite LAPD Unit Disproportionately Stopped Black Drivers, Data Show' (online). Available at: https://www.latimes.com/local/lanow/la-me-lapd-traffic-stops-20190124-story.html (accessed 11 March 2020).

McCord, J., Widom, C., and Crowell, N. 2001. *Juvenile Crime, Juvenile Justice*. Washington, DC: National Academy Press.

Miller, L. 2020. 'The LAPD Branded Them as Gang Associates: But They Fought Back and Got Removed from Calgang Database'. *Los Angeles Times* (online). Available at: https://www.latimes.com/california/story/2020-02-13/california-gang-database-lapd-calgang (accessed 11 February 2020).

Mok, P. L. H., Antonsen, S., Pedersen, C. B., Carr, M. J., Kapur, N., Nazroo, J., and Webb, R. T. 2018. 'Family Income Inequalities and Trajectories through Childhood and Self-Harm and Violence in Young Adults: A Population-Based, Nested Case-Control Study'. *Lancet Public Health*, 3(10), e498–e507.

Porio, E., and Crisol, C. 2004. 'The Use of Children in the Production, Sales and Trafficking of Drugs: A Synthesis of Participatory Action-Oriented Research Programs in Indonesia, the Philippines and Thailand' (online). Available at: https://www.ilo.org/wcmsp5/groups/public/---asia/---ro-bangkok/documents/publication/wcms_bk_pb_24_en.pdf (accessed 4 January 2020).

Prison Law Office. 2016. 'SB 260 and 261 – Youthful Offender Parole Hearings' (online). Available at: http://prisonlaw.com/wp-content/uploads/2016/05/SB-260-261-Youth-Offender-Parole-Guide-w-ltr.pdf (accessed 12 January 2020).

Rodriguez, Stephen G., et al., 2020. 'Gang Enhancement: Legal Dictionary' (online). Available at: https://www.lacriminaldefenseattorney.com/legal-dictionary/g/gang-enhancement/ (accessed 12 March 2020).

Sanchez-Jankowski, M. 2003. 'Gangs and Social Change'. *Theoretical Criminology*, 7(2), 191–216 (online). Available at: https://www.researchgate.net/publication/249720861_Gangs_and_Social_Change (accessed 15 November 2019).

Schmitt, J., and Zipperer, B. 2006. 'Is the U.S. a Good Model for Reducing Social Exclusion in Europe?' (online). Available at: http://cepr.net/documents/social_exclusion_2006_08.pdf (accessed 20 January 2020).

Schools & Communities First. 2020. (Online) Available at: https://www.schoolsandcommunitiesfirst.org/ (accessed 5 March 2020).

Swaine, J., and McCarthy, C. 2017. 'Young Black Men Again Faced Highest Rate of US Police Killings in 2016'. *Guardian* (online). Available at: https://www.theguardian.com/us-news/2017/jan/08/the-counted-police-killings-2016-young-black-men (accessed 3 February 2020).

Wheeler, W. 2020. *State of War: MS-13 and El Salvador's World of Violence*. New York: Columbia Global Reports.

Chapter 7

AFRICAN CONTINENTAL YOUTH POLICY AS A TOOL FOR HARNESSING THE DEMOGRAPHIC DIVIDEND

Patrick Mpedzisi and Annegret Warth

Africa's potential, its opportunity and its rise has long been the fascination of development practitioners, academicians and diplomats. More recently, narratives have picked up on various economic trends that identify sustained economic growth patterns outpacing the rest of the globe. One highly contentious and enthralling narrative due to its double-edged nature is the possibility that the rapid population growth Africa is experiencing can result in a positive outcome for the continent, despite its undeniable threat to the continent and the globe if not managed effectively.

This narrative is framed by the term 'demographic dividend' (DD). It refers to accelerated economic growth, which is initiated by a rapid increase in fertility and decline in mortality resulting in a change in the age structure. This change can lead to an economic dividend, if among other factors, those affected countries are able to navigate from being dominated by dependent children to being dominated by economically productive working adults. In other words, DD can be defined as 'the rise in gross domestic product (GDP) per capita that can result from an increasing proportion of effective income-earners relative to the number of consumers in a population due to shifts in the population age structure and to enhanced productivity resulting from investments in health, empowerment, education and employment' (UNFPA, 2018, p. 10). The UNFPA also remarks that the global DD started in 1973 and is projected to continue until 2026. However, in Africa, the DD started in 1991 and, according to current population projections, will continue until 2083 (p. 10). Presently, Africa is the only region in the world where the youth population is still increasing (see Figure 7.1).

According to the UN, in 2015, 226 million youth aged 15–24 lived in Africa, accounting for 19 per cent of the global youth population. Between

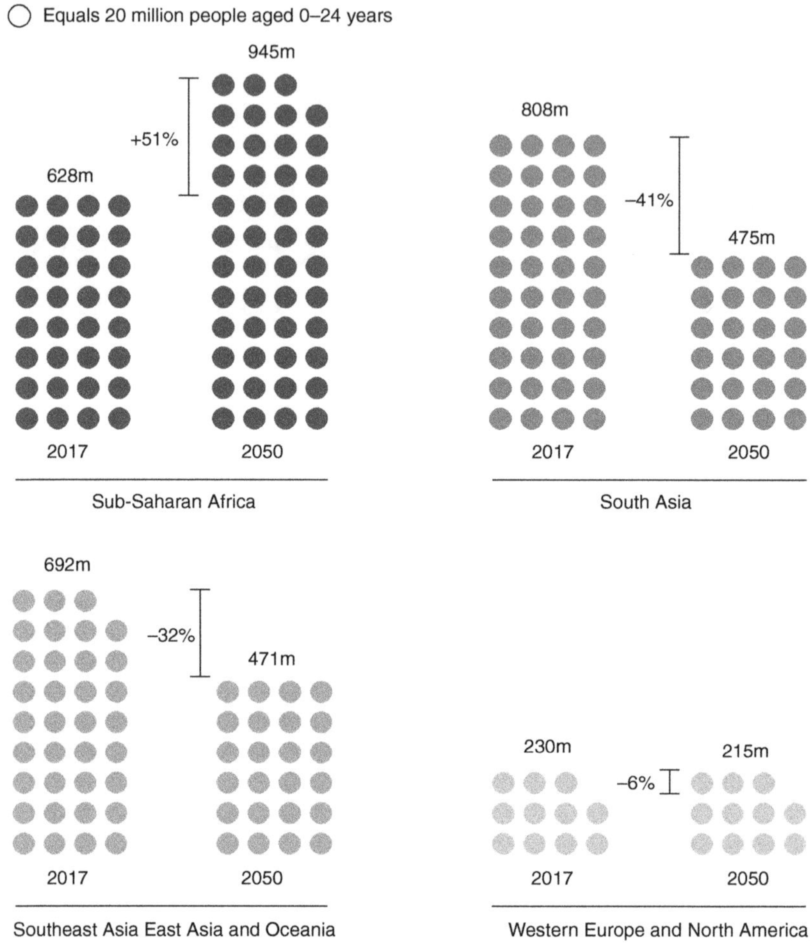

Figure 7.1 Increasing youth population in Africa (IHME, 2018, p. 9).

2017 and 2050, it is projected that the number of youth in Africa will increase by 51 per cent (Sow, 2018). The International Monetary Fund (IMF) estimates that Africa will account for 80 per cent of the increase in the global population, and it is expected to have a population of about 10 billion by 2100 (Drummond et al., 2014, p. 4). The African Development Bank estimates an increase in the youth population of 42 per cent, from 226 million in 2015 to 321 million in 2030 (2018, p. xv).

The current state and projected rise of the youth population in African countries can be traced back to 'decades of very high fertility in Africa, coupled with rapidly declining child mortality' (AFIDEP, 2018, p. xi). However, the benefits of the DD are not an automatic consequence of demographic trends. For releasing that potential, 'countries need to make concerted efforts to implement social and economic policies' (UNFPA, 2018, p. 10). The population growth needs to be aligned with economic opportunities for youth to avoid what is termed a 'youth bulge' – a concept that refers to a situation where there will be no jobs available for the burgeoning youth population. While it is difficult to contain an impending 'youth bulge', the aspiration of the African Union (AU) is to translate this into a DD with effective investments in African youth to bolster economic growth and development.

Youth policies are therefore a strategic policy area for harnessing the DD. Against this backdrop, this chapter aims to introduce international stakeholders to the current challenges and opportunities vis-à-vis African continental youth policy frameworks. First, the evolution and current state of youth policy frameworks on the African continent will be analysed. The AU has put efforts in developing continental youth policy strategies since the beginning of the 2000s. Remarkably, the DD had become the central outlook for youth programming at the continental level by 2017. Second, the chapter addresses three challenges and opportunities vis-à-vis international corporations to harness the DD. International stakeholders cooperating on youth issues can take up the challenge of harmonisation of continental youth policies at national levels by (1) supporting the mainstreaming and harmonisation of the most recent continental youth policies; (2) supporting youth policy monitoring; and (3) strengthening youth representation structures.

Continental Youth Policy and the Demographic Dividend

Through the three main continental youth policy documents, one can trace the growing interest of the AU in youth matters and its growing urgency around this demographic. The African Youth Charter (AYC; AU, 2006), the Youth Decade Plan of Action 2009–2018 (DPoA; AU, 2011) and the AU Roadmap on Harnessing the Demographic Dividend through Investments in Youth (AU, 2017) illustrate the process of addressing youth as a policy category with the AYC (AU, 2006) and subsequently aligning and prioritising youth policy issues within the context of the DD (AU, 2011; 2017). As a starting premise, it will be important to review their main topics and their relation to the framework of the DD.

The AYC (AU, 2006) is the first continental policy paper that explicitly addresses youth as a prioritised policy area. It was endorsed on 2 July 2006 at the African Union Heads of States and Governments meeting in Banjul, the Gambia, and it entered into force on 8 August 2009 with the 15 required ratifications received. The AYC underscores the importance of youth development in the AU's development agenda and acknowledges the situation of youth in Africa, many of whom have been marginalised by society through wealth and power inequalities, poor quality of education, limited health care, unemployment and exposure to violence among other challenges identified. Its content is based on a human rights approach. Its 26 articles define 'rights and duties' of youth, which cover a wide range of policy areas, amongst others, employment, sustainable livelihoods, education, health, youth participation, peace and security, law enforcement, youth in the diaspora and youth with disabilities. The charter seeks to guarantee a comprehensive set of rights to the continent's youth such as freedom of movement, expression, association, conscience and privacy, the protection of family life, the right to hold property, the right to education and training, as well as the right to protection and due consideration of the law.

The AYC is a political and legal document that serves as the strategic framework for African states, giving direction for youth empowerment and development at the continental, regional and national levels. It is a clear expression that youth were regarded as an important policy issue in Africa at the beginning of the 2000s. However, at the time of its development, it did not explicitly relate youth policy to the concept of DD.

Subsequent to the AYC, the AU adopted the DPoA (AU, 2011). The existence of the DPoA underscores the priority of youth policy in Africa at the beginning of the 2010s: 'Africa needs deliberate efforts to accelerate social development that give high priority to youth empowerment and development' (p. vii). It is predominantly a technical policy paper that addresses policies and legislations, programmes and plans, institutional capacity and mobilising resources, as well as monitoring and evaluation outcomes, the widespread challenge of implementing the AYC, in four implementation areas (pp. 7–13). Furthermore, crucial for implementation are the 'multi-sectoral and multi-dimensional engagement' (p. i) of various stakeholders on international, continental, national and local levels and standardised and evidence-based data collection and monitoring tools to measure the effectiveness and efficiency of youth policies.

The DPoA furthermore prioritises the previous 25 policy areas to 5 thematic areas of 'education, health, employment & income, poverty, participation' (p. 17) and underlines 'youth participation as an epicenter of socio-economic investments' (p. 14). Remarkably, the DPoA expands the meaning of youth as a policy category. It states that Africa's youth population is no longer simply a political force that needs to be accommodated in national planning. Rather the current population growth could lead to an important economic force or threaten stability if not fully addressed: 'The DPoA is both a framework and a vehicle for addressing Africa's development challenges through mobilizing sustained, concerted and requisite investment in the potential of the continents youth recognized as a demographic [dividend]' (p. 14). Essentially, this is the policy that introduces the concept of demographic bonus (dividend) into AU youth frameworks and highlights the urgency of the issue through a deliberate effort to secure greater implementation.

Furthermore, Agenda 2063 (AU, 2013) maintains a pattern of thriving not only for youth policy implementation but also urgency around monitoring this implementation. The Agenda notes that 'past development experience, review of national plans and implementation of continental frameworks indicate the need for a Monitoring and Evaluation framework to be part of the Agenda 2063 implementation' (p. 97). Agenda 2063 is the continental master plan for Africa for the next 50 years, and it refocuses and reprioritises Africa's agenda from the attainment of political independence (the foundation of the Organization of African Unity – now known as the AU) to sustainable development for all. One of the seven aspirations of Agenda 2063 points to the relevance of women, youth and children for development in African countries (p. 76).

Agenda 2063 reinforces the realisation and mainstreaming of the AYC, by programming the subsequent implementation phase of the DPoA by a 'Five Year Plan of Action on Youth Empowerment' (2019–24). New here is the definition of regional and national indicators next to the already formulated continental actions (pp. 78–79). Agenda 2063 supports the role of monitoring implementation at national, regional and continental levels within 10-year implementation phases which highlight key targets and indicators such as integrating the continental Plan of Action on Youth Empowerment into national and regional planning frameworks by 2019/2020 (p. 79).

The development policy discourse framed by the DD finally became the centre of continental African Youth Policies through the same titled theme of the 2017 AU summit and its 'Roadmap on Harnessing the Demographic Dividend through Investments in Youth' (AU, 2017). This policy paper reframes and condenses the prior youth policy of the AYC (AU, 2006). It addresses youth policy as a tool to harness the DD in Africa and acknowledges the need for development and implementation of sound policies to ensure the increase of productive workforce, leading to higher growth and rising income per person. While the AYC targets youth policy in a way that is very comprehensive in its scope but lacks analytical clarity, the AU Roadmap of 2017 presents consistent and prioritised interventions.

This new generation of African youth policies displays an integrated policy strategy containing the four widely acknowledged (AFIDEP, 2018; PRB, 2017) policy areas of Education and Skills Development, Employment and Entrepreneurship, Health and Well-being, and Rights, Governance and Youth Empowerment, which are appropriated by 49 key actions and deliverables. This is often referred to as the 4E's of education, employment, entrepreneurship and empowerment. These 4E's are often found in national youth policies developed since 2011 such as the Zambian Youth Policy (Republic of Zambia, 2015), the Mauritian Youth Policy (Republic of Mauritius, 2016), the revised Malawi Youth Policy (Republic of Malawi, 2013) and others that are still in the formulation stage such as Sierra Leone (National Youth Commission Sierra Leone, 2012).

The aforementioned three main youth policy documents show the evolution of youth as a policy category in continental African policymaking and their further development and harmonisation to global policy discourses, such as the DD, Agenda 2063 as well as more recently, the Sustainable Development Goals of the Agenda 2030. As the DPoA explicitly points out, implementation on continental, regional, national and even local levels remains a major challenge to the elaborated and progressive policy development at the continental level. Presently, 42 AU member states have signed and 38 member states have ratified the charter (see Figure 7.2).

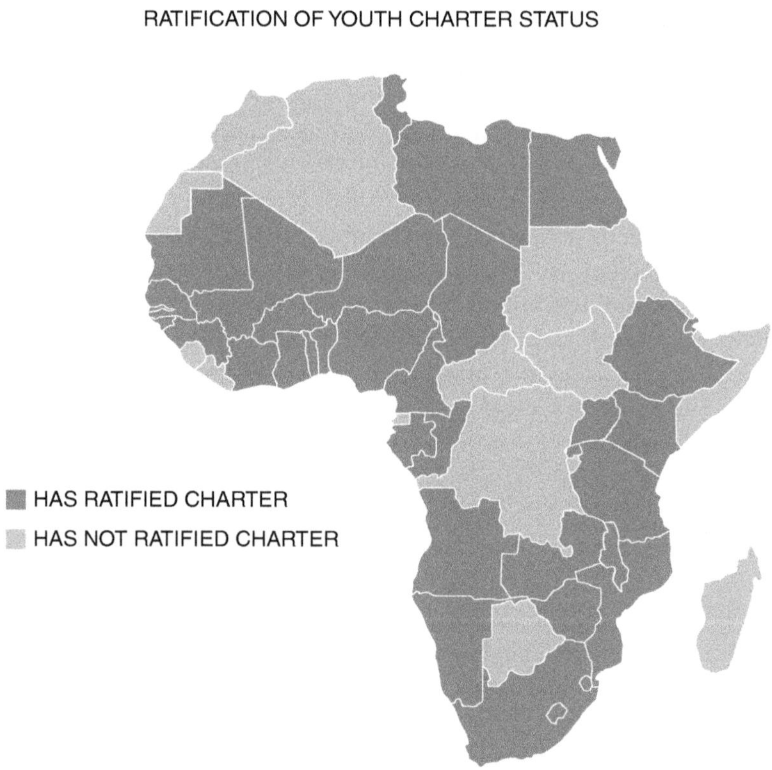

Figure 7.2 Ratification status of the AYC as of 2019 (AUC/PRB, 2019, p. 8).

Since 2006, Africa has witnessed a momentum of progressive reframing of continental youth policies from simply a legal and policy document for the participation and empowerment of youth to meta policy frameworks such as the DD and the SDGs. They imply the establishment of new, and the redefinition of existing, policymaking institutions and structures. The AU Initiative '1 Million By 2021' (AU, 2019), the Status of Africa Youth Report (SoAYR; AUC/PRB, 2019) and the AU Youth Envoy are three examples. Many stakeholders have contributed to this, including international partners, intergovernmental bodies, member states themselves and a multiplicity of stakeholders at various levels.

Challenges and Opportunities of International Corporations to Harness the Demographic Dividend in the Context of Youth Policy

Following these assumptions, this chapter concludes with respective suggestions for international cooperation regarding the following three challenges:

1. Support the mainstreaming and harmonisation of continental youth policies

Currently, the AYC (AU, 2006) sets the standard for the youth policy making and various youth policies established after its coming into force. More than 30 of the 55 African states have passed a national youth policy (AUC/PRB, 2019, p. 9), and since the advent of the AYC, many countries have embarked on a revision of their youth policies. The analysis of the collected national youth policy papers of African states by the German think tank Youth Policy Labs (youthpolicy.org) shows most of them had been adopted in the 2000s until 2013. However in view of the progression at the continental level to viewing youth as potential DD (AU, 2017), national youth policies need to take the same route as continental youth policies and reframe and reprioritise their national youth policies in line with continental youth policy frameworks. This remains a challenge of the AU architecture in that regional economic communities (RECs) and the member states are slow to respond to key continental challenges and opportunities identified at the AU level. It is not clear to which extent the RECs have also aligned with the AU on how they support it in monitoring their member states' commitment to their youth. Furthermore, the AU Youth Policy Papers subsequent to the AYC are not known at the local level, and therefore, many civil society organisations are not actively following up on the implementation of these frameworks at the national, regional or continental level.

Recommendation: Ani (2018, p. 8) accepts the 'uncertainty of external support' which still dominates the financing of AU interventions and therefore "'entails that African bodies are also restricted in making tangible and binding decisions unless their decisions are accepted and funded by external donors'. It is therefore critical that international stakeholders support the harmonisation process of DD-related youth policies by aligning to the AU Roadmap of 2017 and using the 4E's, namely education, employment, entrepreneurship and empowerment, as a strategic framework in international cooperation.

2. Support youth policy monitoring on local, national and continental levels

Data creation and access to data in the process of AU youth policy implementation is another challenge. Without access to information and data at all levels, it is difficult for multisector stakeholders to appreciate the urgency of youth policy implementation and hold their governments and the AU accountable. At the continental level, the African Peer Review Mechanism (APRM) is a mutually agreed instrument voluntarily acceded to by AU member states as an African self-monitoring mechanism reform. The APRM provides very clear modalities for monitoring the implementation of AU decisions. Recently, it was declared as a central 'monitoring and evaluation role for the African Union Agenda 2063 and the United Nations Sustainable Development Goals Agenda 2030' (AU, 2018a, p. 134).

The country review reports (CRRs) of the APRM are key for monitoring the implementation of the AU policy frameworks vis-à-vis the youth. However, these reports are either not available or not made public for all stakeholders. Meta-analysis of the accessible CRRs (Corrigan, 2016a,b) nevertheless illustrates that APRM's enquiries are of great value for gaining an overview on youth policy development in the participating African countries. In line with the AU decision in 2017 (AU, 2018a), it is now possible to enhance the indicators for youth policy in line with the DD.

Recommendation: International stakeholders can support youth policy monitoring by first recognising the APRM's potential as a continental youth policy monitoring mechanism. Second, international cooperation should aim at empowering national and local stakeholders such as the media, youth organisations, universities and think tanks for monitoring activities to support data creation for the CRRs of the APRM.

3. Strengthen youth representation structures

Youth participation in the development and implementation of youth policy structures is one of the 4E's of the AU Roadmap on Harnessing the DD

(AU, 2017). Establishing credible and legitimate youth structures, especially at the continental and regional levels and in some national contexts, remains a challenge. On the continental level, the AU originally worked with the Pan African Youth Union (PYU) in the process of the implementation of the AYC. However, in January 2018, the AU issued the following statement: 'The AUC confirms its full de-association from the PYU and that it does not recognize the current executive committee' (AU, 2018b). While it is commendable that the African Union Commission took a stand to disassociate itself from values that are inconsistent with its own, the lack of a recognised representative youth structure still leaves a vacuum for follow-up and implementation. Such a structure is meant to assist and facilitate in the implementation of AU decisions for youth by monitoring at the AU and national levels. The same structure would then set up other structures at the regional economic committees to further ensure coherence with the national and continental levels. The establishment of an AU Youth Envoy – an initiative founded in 2019 to connect African youth with the AU and enhance youth leadership and participation – while commendable, is not sufficient for ensuring that member states are held accountable to their commitments under the AYC, the DPoA and the Roadmap for Harnessing the DD.

Recommendation: To harness the DD in African countries, substantial policy planning, implementation and investment at all levels is required. In the past 10 years, youth policies have been progressively reformulated to the framework of the DD. A major risk for harnessing the dividend is the extent to which national and regional youth policy frameworks can align and harmonise with the continental architecture as well as the extent to which implementation can be strictly adhered to. International stakeholders cooperating on youth issues have the opportunity to take up the challenge by supporting the mainstreaming and harmonisation of the most recent continental youth policies and reinforcing youth policy monitoring as well as strengthening youth representation structures.

References

AFIDEP. 2018. 'East African Regional Analysis of Youth Demographics'. Available at: https://www.afidep.org/2018-2019-kenya-national-budget-investing-in-youth/ (accessed 17 December 2019).

African Development Bank. 2018. 'African Outlook Report'. Available at: https://www.afdb.org/fileadmin/uploads/afdb/Documents/Publications/African_Economic_Outlook_2018_-_EN.pdf (accessed 6 January 2020).

Amupanda, Job Shipululo. 2018. 'The African Union (AU), the African Youth Commission (AYC) and the Pan-African Youth Union (PYU): Sabotaging or Bureaucratizing the Youth?' In *Stichproben. Wiener Zeitschrift für kritische Afrikastudien*, no. 35/2018, vol. 18, pp. 73–82. Available at: http://repository.unam.edu.na/bitstream/handle/11070/2500/amupanda_au_2018.pdf?sequence=1&isAllowed=y (accessed 7 January 2020).

Ani, Ndubuisi. 2018. 'Three Schools of Thought on "African Solutions to African Problems"'. *Journal of Black Studies* 50(2), 135–55.

AU. 2006. 'African Youth Charter'. Available at: https://au.int/en/treaties/african-youth-charter (accessed 19 December 2019).

———. 2011. 'African Youth Decade 2009–2018 Plan of Action'. Available at: https://www.youthpolicy.org/wp-content/uploads/library/2011_African_Youth_Decade_Plan_Action_2009-2018_Eng1.pdf (accessed 5 January 2020).

———. 2013. 'AGENDA 2063. The Africa We Want. A Shared Strategic Framework for Inclusive Growth and Sustainable Development'. Available at: https://www.un.org/en/africa/osaa/pdf/au/agenda2063-first10yearimplementation.pdf (accessed 19 December 2019).

———. 2017. 'AU Roadmap on Harnessing the Demographic Dividend through Investments in Youth, in Response to AU Assembly Decision (Assembly/AU/Dec.601 (XXVI))'. Available at: https://wcaro.unfpa.org/sites/default/files/pub-pdf/AU%202017%20DD%20ROADMAP%20Final%20-%20EN.pdf (accessed 19 December 2019).

———. 2018a. 'Assembly of the Union, Twenty-Eighth Ordinary Session, 30–31 January 2017'. Available at: https://au.int/sites/default/files/decisions/32520-sc19553_e_original_-_assembly_decisions_621-641_-_xxviii.pdf (accessed 7 January 2020).

———. 2018b. 'Statement of the African Union (AU) on the Elections of the Pan African Youth Forum (PYU)'. Available at: https://au.int/sites/default/files/pressreleases/33602-pr-statement_of_au_final_corrections_18_01_2018-2.pdf (accessed 7 January 2020).

———. 2019. '1 Million by 2021 Initiative Communications Toolkit'. Available at: https://en.unesco.org/sites/default/files/1mby2021communicationstoolkit.pdf (accessed 22 December 2019).

AUC/PRB. 2019. 'Africa's Future: Youth and the Data Defining Their Lives'. Policy Brief. Available at: https://au.int/en/documents/20191204/africas-future-youth-and-data-defining-their-lives (accessed 22 December 2019).

National Youth Commission Sierra Leone. 2012. 'Review of the Sierra Leone National Youth Policy'. Available at: https://www.youthpolicy.org/library/wp-content/uploads/library/2012_Sierra_Leone_Youth_Report.pdf (accessed 22 December 2019).

Corrigan, Terence. 2016a. 'What Ails the Young? Insights into Africa's Youth from The African Peer Review Mechanism'. Occasional Policy Paper 234, South African Institute of International Affairs (SAIIA). Available at: https://saiia.org.za/research/what-ails-the-young-insights-into-africas-youth-from-the-african-peer-review-mechanism/ (accessed 10 November 2019).

———. 2016b. 'Successful Youth Policy: Lessons from the African Peer Review Mechanism'. Policy Briefing 149, South African Institute of International Affairs (SAIIA), Available at: https://saiia.org.za/research/successful-youth-policy-lessons-from-the-african-peer-review-mechanism/ (accessed 10 November 2019).

Drummond, Paulo, Thakoor, Vimal, and Yu, Shu Yu. 2014. 'Africa Rising: Harnessing the Demographic Dividend'. IMF Working Paper. Available at: https://www.imf.org/en/Publications/WP/Issues/2016/12/31/Africa-Rising-Harnessing-the-Demographic-Dividend-41819 (accessed 10 November 2019).

Institute for Health Metrics and Evaluation (IHME). 2018. 'Goalkeepers Report'. Available at: https://www.gatesfoundation.org/goalkeepers/report/2018-report?download=false (accessed 10 November 2019).

PRB (Population Reference Bureau). 2017. 'The Demographic Dividend in Africa Relies on Investments in the Reproductive Health and Rights of Adolescents and Youth'. Policy brief. Available at: https://www.prb.org/african-demographic-dividend/ (accessed 10 November 2020).

Republic of Malawi. 2013. 'National Youth Policy'. Available at: https://youthpolicy.org/national/Malawi_2013_National_Youth_Policy.pdf (accessed 10 November 2019).

Republic of Mauritius. 2016. 'National Youth Policy'. Available at: http://mys.govmu.org/English/Documents/National%20Youth%20Policy/NYP2016.pdf (accessed 10 November 2019).

Republic of Zambia. 2015. '2015 National Youth Policy'. Available at: https://www.ilo.org/wcmsp5/groups/public/---ed_emp/---ed_emp_msu/documents/projectdocumentation/wcms_427020.pdf (accessed 10 November 2019).

Sow, Mariama. 2018. 'Figures of the Week: Africa's Growing Youth Population and Human Capital Investments'. Available at: https://www.brookings.edu/blog/africa-in-focus/2018/09/20/figures-of-the-week-africas-growing-youth-population-and-human-capital-investments/ (accessed 17 November 2019).

UN. 2015. 'Youth Population Trends and Sustainable Development'. UN Population facts 2015/1. Available at: https://www.un.org/esa/socdev/documents/youth/fact-sheets/YouthPOP.pdf (accessed 10 November 2019).

UNFPA. 2018. 'Programming the Demographic Dividend: from Theory to Experience'. Available at: https://wcaro.unfpa.org/sites/default/files/pub-pdf/unfpa-dividende-en-.pdf (accessed 10 November 2019).

Chapter 8

DIGITAL MINDFULNESS FOR INDIAN MILLENNIALS

Rudrani Dasgupta

India is officially the 'world's most depressed country'. A recent World Health Organisation (WHO) report declared that India displays the highest rates of anxiety, depression and schizophrenia, claiming that at least 6.5 per cent of its population suffers from mental illness (WHO, 2017). This is a crisis and India is right at the centre, with over 50 million depressed Indians in 2015 and the highest number of suicides in 2012. The complex situation is further compounded by the fact that mental health is still a taboo topic in the country, with a lack of an active public discourse. The year 2020, with the ongoing pandemic and subsequent lockdown, might just prove to be the proverbial straw on the camel's back, as reported mental health cases have seen a steep rise by 20 per cent since the lockdown was imposed in India, according to a study by the Indian Psychiatric Society in April 2020 (Andrade, 2020).

By 2020, India is set to become the world's 'youngest country' with 64 per cent of its population being of working age. However, the COVID-19 pandemic and its subsequent contractive effects on local and global economies present critical challenges in terms of economic opportunities for the young working population. An International Labour Organisation (ILO) report in May 2020 stated that over one in six people aged 29 have lost their jobs due to the pandemic and that young people are being severely affected due to disruption in education, employment and training.

Young people are already being disproportionately affected by mental health problems. WHO data pegs suicide as the second leading cause of death among 15- to 29-year-olds, with 79 per cent of global suicides happening in low- to middle-income countries like India. Multiple shocks are bound to have critical repercussions on the Indian youth population.

The burden of this mental health crisis is multifold: it has a tremendous impact on individual well-being, on productivity and, ultimately, on society and the economy. At this juncture, the question about the extent to which India can truly reap the benefits of the demographic dividend is still relevant. Especially if its population is not mentally healthy and affordable mental healthcare remains, by and large, inaccessible, particularly at a time when the world is reeling under an unprecedented crisis.

The Mindfulness Market

Any industry catering to the needs of the youth population is likely to be a profitable venture. As of 2019, 16 per cent of the world's population is between the ages of 15 and 24, according to the UN DESA (United Nations Department of Economic and Social Affairs; UN, 2018). There is an evident gap in mental health services and, as usual, the market-driven economy has a solution. Technology has often aimed to plug market gaps for essential services; it was only a matter of time before digital solutions to the mental health and wellness crisis were developed. Using age-old practices of meditation and mindfulness, the past eight to nine years have been a turning point for the wellness industry, with the rise of quasi-spiritual leaders like former monks Jay Shetty and Andy Puddicombe and an increasing repertoire of meditation apps, such as Headspace, Calm and Smiling Mind, catering to a largely millennial demographic.

With a rapidly developing youth demographic dealing with the stresses of the economy, India has been tagged as the perfect market for wellness solutions. Unsurprisingly, China, Brazil, the United States, India and Indonesia are the top five players in the beauty and wellness market (KPMG and NSDC, 2017). There is an increased industry focus on the burgeoning Indian wellness market. A 2016 report by the Federation of Indian Chambers of Commerce & Industry (FICCI) and Ernst & Young estimated that the wellness industry would grow at a compounded rate of 12 per cent and hit UD$1.5 trillion by 2020 (FICCI, 2020). According to the report, increasing disposable incomes, higher stress levels in tier-1 cities and emerging awareness of mental health and holistic well-being are some of the key drivers of the industry. Home-grown Indian wellness apps such as Sattva and Black Lotus are gaining momentum as increasing numbers of young Indians are subscribing to such apps to focus on their well-being. Most Indian apps are developed as offshoots of popular spiritual 'guru-led' movements, differing from the non-denominational models of Headspace and the like.

The investment numbers are indicative of an upward demand among young working people for digital wellness solutions. According to Pitchbook (Olsen, 2018), the number of mental health start-ups funded by venture capital investors jumped from 7 to 30 between 2009 and 2018. Calm is a darling of venture capital firms, having just raised US$143 million till 2019. Globally, meditation apps are part of a burgeoning multimillion-dollar wellness industry which has made a clear shift from niche to mainstream. The first such popular app in the market was Insight Timer, founded by Brad Fullmer in 2010 as the first 'social meditation app'. Started in 2012, Headspace has since raised a total of US$215.9 million up to June 2020 with two million subscribers. Celebrities such as Ashton Kutcher, Harry Styles and Jessica Alba are early investors in these apps. Clearly, meditation and mindfulness are shedding their tie-dye 'hippie' associations and mean serious business.

Indian Millennials and Mental Health: Anecdotes

Madhumita Bhattacharya, a Bengaluru-based author, feels that building a meditation practice, given its well-documented effects, would give her a certain energy. Someone had recommended Headspace to her, and she had enjoyed the short, guided meditation sessions as they led her to understand the importance of being a mindful parent. Meditation apps such as Headspace offer short, guided meditation sessions and courses to deal with issues such as stress and anxiety. Users follow guided exercises that teach people mindful practices, using a combination of breathing exercises and verbal instructions. Kritisha, a communication designer, used meditation apps for a year to start her own meditation practice.

For the purposes of this chapter, many Indian men were willing to talk about their experiences battling mental health problems. Broadly in their late twenties to mid-thirties and living in metro cities, the demographic is largely sector agnostic. From visual artists to IT and tech consultants, no one is immune from stress. Riasat from Mumbai believes that it's not just workplace stress, but changing patterns of human behaviour and interactions that cause mental health problems, especially among young people. Many urban millennial men were very open about struggles with mental health, engaging in discussions in their circles.

Mental health is largely perceived as a feminised issue. Past studies, including one by MacLean et al. (2012), highlight how 'help seeking' and mental health vary noticeably by gender; girls and women are more likely to self-report mental health problems as opposed to men. This is largely underpinned by gender stereotypes of masculinity and how men are expected to be 'stronger'. Anecdotally, there seems to be an increasing awareness of the culture of silence that generally discourages men from seeking help on emotional and psychological struggles.

The Relevance of Digital Mindfulness

With quick 10-minute sessions and quirky infographics, these apps are attractive to newcomers. Dr Divya Kannan, a clinical psychologist, thinks that these digital tools empower her clients to learn new skills and recognise when they might be in need of these practices. Some users mentioned that they were nudged into using these apps as a coping mechanism to deal with depression or anxiety. The question remains as to how effective these apps are in combating specific mental health issues.

Multiple studies have been conducted on testing the effectiveness of mental health apps, including an RCT (randomised controlled trial) in 2016 (Howells et al., 2014), with 121 adults assigned to use Headspace or an attention control app. The participants reported an improvement in their positive emotions and depressive symptoms after 10 days. Yet another RCT conducted with college students on the use of mental health apps Smiling Mind and Headspace reported a small yet statistically significant decrease in depressive symptoms, increase in resilience and greater adjustment to college life. However, the study (Flett et al., 2018) did report a significant drop in use across the time period. However, both the studies did not record any significant change in the life satisfaction or 'flourishing' among participants, suggesting that long-term studies are required to fully understand the impact of long-term usage of these apps. Research remains emergent as the role of multiple variables, casualties and correlations need to be explored.

Mental health experts advise caution before turning to these apps as a silver bullet for actual problems. Prarthana Prakash, a psychologist, thinks that these solutions should be seen as tools, not actual interventions. Apps are often recommended by therapists as one of a set of tools or as 'homework' exercises; depending on the patient's profile, at a point called the 'working stage' in the therapy process. Apps offer general self-help advice but no tailored solutions for people suffering from mental health problems. Every case is unique and requires conceptualisation and a tailored methodology, Prakash underlined.

A psychologist and professor from Pune says that these apps offer guidance through monologues: this could be potentially dangerous as people are vulnerable and open to suggestion; clients cannot debate and counter suggestions handed out, unlike with actual therapists. According to these experts, such apps with their subscription models can breed dependency among users. There is no accountability as in therapeutic interventions and trust forming is crucial. Therapy is about setting a goal with your therapist and actively working towards it – an experience that apps are unable to offer.

In spite of the booming subscriber numbers during this pandemic, just how consistent is the usage graph? Is this trend just a flash in the pan or indicative of a significant shift towards mental well-being amidst turbulent times? Estimates by app intelligence firm Sensor Tower show over two million more downloads of top meditation apps in April 2020 as compared to January of the same year. The top 10 apps, including Calm and Headspace, generated a 24.2 per cent increase in downloads in April as compared to January. It is to be noted that this data is not age-specific (Chapple, 2020). Most users find it difficult to stick to a daily routine, as observed in an RCT study. While investors are no longer shy of pouring in millions of dollars into recreating 'authentic' meditation experiences to attract millennials surviving with inaccessible mental health services, the jury is still out on whether this trend will sustain with young Indians.

Alternative Solutions

Anecdotal evidence points to how the lack of affordable and accessible mental health resources is pushing an ever-growing population of young people towards temporary solutions. Globally and locally, access to affordable quality mental health services continues to be a problem. The number of psychiatrists per 100,000 Indians varies between 0.05 to 1.2, according to a study conducted by the National Institute of Mental Health and Neuro-Sciences in 2015–16 in 12 of the 29 states of India. Affordable treatment options are inaccessible to the wider population. Therapy is expensive and often consistent sessions become unsustainable. A session could cost between INR 1,000 and 5,000 (US$14–70) in most Indian cities.

Further, it is not merely the lack of solutions but the absence of a fully formed discourse on mental health as a critical component of health and well-being. Prarthana and the professor from Pune agree that lack of accessible and affordable therapists could possibly be pushing people into 'self-help' using meditation apps.

First, the government should take concrete steps to increase investment in mental healthcare facilities and implement subsidised mental healthcare solutions across the country. Currently, India's mental health budget (Union Budget, 2020) stands at a paltry 0.05 per cent of the total healthcare budget for 2020. Mental healthcare legislation should be strongly operationalised and budget allocations for the national mental health programmes should be increased so that there is equity of access. Large-scale and widespread campaigning for increased awareness on mental health is crucial, especially in schools, colleges and workplaces, to bring about behavioural changes in communities that have long stigmatised mental health issues as taboo.

Second, civil society organisations can play an elemental role in lobbying and advocating with governments, corporations, educational bodies and other power structures to mainstream mental health in their respective contexts. It is high time that mental health emerges from the shadows and whispers to become a socio-developmental priority in the country. Until then, Indian millennials will continue to depend on ad hoc solutions for their mental well-being. In light of the ongoing pandemic, the existing mental health infrastructure in India needs to be suitably shored up to deal with the challenges that lie ahead. Without critical policy commitments and investments, the Indian demographic dividend will remain underutilised as young people continue to reel under the mental stresses brought on by the multiple shocks of the pandemic and an economy in crisis.

References

Andrade, C. 2020. 'COVID-19 and Lockdown: Delayed Effects on Health'. http://www.indianjpsychiatry.org/text.asp?2020/62/3/247/284459.

Chapple, C. 2020. 'Downloads of Top English-Language Mental Wellness Apps Surged by 2 Million in April Amid COVID-19 Pandemic'. Sensor Tower. https://sensortower.com/blog/top-mental-wellness-apps-april-2020-downloads.

FICCI. 2020. 'Indian Wellness Industry Likely to Hit Rs 1.5 Trillion by FY 2019–20: Report'. LiveMint, 31 January (online). Available at: http://www.ficci.in/ficci-in-news-page.asp?nid=12178.

Flett, J. A. M., Hayne, H., Riordan, B. C., Thompson, L. M., and Conner, T. S. 2018. 'Mobile Mindfulness Meditation: A Randomised Controlled Trial of the Effect of Two Popular Apps on Mental Health'. *Mindfulness* 10(5): 863–76. doi:10.1007/s12671-018-1050-9.

Howells, A., Ivtzan, I., and Eiroa-Orosa, F. J. 2014. 'Putting the "App" in Happiness: A Randomised Controlled Trial of a Smartphone-Based Mindfulness Intervention to Enhance Wellbeing'. *Journal of Happiness Studies* 17(1): 163–85. doi:10.1007/s10902-014-9589-1.

International Labour Organisation. 2020. 'COVID-19 and the World of Work: Fourth Edition Updated Estimates and Analysis'. ILO Monitor. https://www.ilo.org/wcmsp5/groups/public/---dgreports/---dcomm/documents/briefingnote/wcms_745963.pdf.

KPMG Advisory Services Pvt. Ltd. 2017. 'Human Resource and Skill Requirements in the Beauty and Wellness Sector'. National Skill Development Corporation (online). Available at: https://nsdcindia.org/sites/default/files/Beauty-Wellness.pdf.

MacLean, A., Hunt, K., and Sweeting, H. 2012. 'Symptoms of Mental Health Problems: Children's and Adolescents' Understandings and Implications for Gender Differences in Help Seeking'. *Children & Society* 27(3): 161–73.

National Institute of Mental Health and Neuro-Sciences Bengaluru. 2016. *National Mental Health Survey of India, 2015–16*. Bengaluru: NIMHANS.

Olsen, D. 2018. 'A Look at the Boom in VC Funding for Mental Health Startups: Pitchbook'. Pitchbook.com. https://pitchbook.com/news/articles/a-look-at-the-boom-in-vc-funding-for-mental-health-startups.

Union Budget. 2020. Indiabudget.gov.in. https://www.indiabudget.gov.in/.

United Nations. 2018. 'Youth and the 2030 Agenda for Sustainable Development'. World Youth Report. New York: United Nations. https://www.un.org/development/desa/youth/wp-content/uploads/sites/21/2018/12/WorldYouthReport-2030Agenda.pdf.

World Health Organization. 2017. 'Depression and Other Common Mental Disorders: Global Health Estimates' (online). Geneva: World Health Organization. Available at: https://apps.who.int/iris/bitstream/handle/10665/254610/WHO-MSD-MER-2017.2-eng.pdf?sequence=1.

Chapter 9

LESSONS FROM AFRICA: WHAT CAN A COMMUNITY OF PASTORALISTS OFFER THE INTERNATIONAL COOPERATION COMMUNITY?

Elizabeth Maloba and Stefan Cibian

Introduction

In conceptualising this chapter, we have had to recognise that while joint authorship of a chapter usually suggests the writers have an ongoing dialogue arising out of common reading and discussions, this was clearly not the case between us. We live and work on two different continents; our training and backgrounds differ; and our work experience is diverse. And yet, despite these differences, we share common insights. We are guided by the common belief that to be successful in delivering development in Africa, the international community has to move beyond Western conceptual frames and embrace the sociocultural institutions and practices that have enabled Africans to survive for centuries.

There are many reasons for our collaboration on this chapter. One is to make visible the 'other', local, sociocultural processes that are becoming increasingly invisible as the Western world order appears to spread across the continent. Another is the optimistic belief that embracing these local sociocultural processes enables the building of stronger institutions and implementation of sustainable solutions. Our aim is twofold: first, to show that while invisible, it is these processes that often represent drivers of stability, development and sustainability; and second, to call for an increase in visibility and recognition, by connecting these processes with development efforts across the continent. It is our conviction that by recognising local sociocultural processes, we find new and more effective solutions to challenges such as population dynamics or protracted conflicts.

This chapter is informed by our basic understanding of inclusion as an approach that leads to ownership, innovation and sustainability. In the following pages, we start by examining the concepts of development cooperation and demographic transition as two basic elements of the process of 'collaboration to achieve a demographic dividend'. We then present a case study of sociocultural practices of pastoral communities that have enabled them to retain stability and generate development for hundreds of years. We find the case of land governance among pastoralist communities to be illustrative of how local ways of life that support communities to be resilient could inspire a different approach to the development of population policy in order for the demographic dividend to have a chance to be realised.

Development Cooperation and the Aid System

Development cooperation is a phenomenon that has existed for decades, part of an international system that is yet to prove its resilience in global problem-solving. Development cooperation is also an industry that brings together actors with different levels of capabilities to address challenges at local, regional and global levels. More than half a century of engagements in development has generated a myriad of actors and cooperation approaches (Acharya et al., 2006); (Knack and Rahman, 2008; OECD, 2011) with limited success to date. Both perceived and observable failure generate enhanced academic debates, policy struggles and political challenges. These encompass a growing criticism towards all actors involved and the overarching global and economic political system (Severino and Ray, 2009, 2010; Moyo, 2009; Kharas and Rogerson, 2012; Alonso, 2012; Sumner and Mallett, 2013; Mawdsley et al., 2014; Kaul et al., 2003; Dingwerth and Pattberg, 2006).

The tensions created by what is perceived to be slow, inefficient and insufficient advancement in development leads to an enduring tension between the global North and the global South, between developed and developing countries. Within this context, aid, the core ingredient of development cooperation, locks the involved stakeholders in a perpetually unequal partnership making the possibility for local ownership and mutual trust illusory. Aid acquires various understandings when disbursed by governments and also when analysed by academics, who look at it from a self-interest, values or moral perspective (Alesina and Dollar, 2000; Berthélemy, 2006; Temple, 2010; Claessens et al., 2007; Headey, 2008; Burnside and Dollar, 2000; Hoeffler and Outram, 2011; Lumsdaine, 1993).

Agenda 2030, the 2015 United Nations Sustainable Development Goals (SDGs), shakes the global development sector in new ways. The SDGs are adopted at a time when the number and size of newly emerging donors generate new forms of development cooperation and South-South partnerships. It is yet to be seen how the pressures coming from new actors in global development – emerging donors and the private sector, and the increasingly introverted Western powers (Petersen, 2011) – are going to affect the aid sector (Kanbur and Sumner, 2012; Kharas and Rogerson, 2012). These changes bring an impact also on 'achieving the demographic dividend in Africa'.

Challenges with development cooperation do not remain at the level of the international community or the Western donors. A wide array of challenges are encountered in the interaction between state and society in sub-Saharan African countries. While African societies expose a great diversity, the political institutions currently in place are often unable to meaningfully connect to local societies. This gap has been explored in the state-society relations literature (Migdal, 1988; Cibian, 2011).

The challenges presented here add up to a convoluted and complex web of dysfunctional relations and misunderstanding, of which the most striking is the inability of Western donors to connect to and understand local and state realities in sub-Saharan Africa (Cibian, 2011).

Demographic Transition

Over time, the world population has continued to grow, from one billion at the beginning of the nineteenth century to seven billion now, with a projection to reach ten billion at the end of the twenty-first century (Worldometers, 2019). However, the rate of growth has been declining, from a high of 2 per cent in the 1960s to a present rate of 1.2 per cent with an expectation of 0 per cent around 2100 (Population Division, United Nations, 2016). Within this overall picture exists a wide range of reality – in Europe the rate has been low since the 1950s and reached 0 at the end of the twentieth century; in Asia and Latin America the rate declined from 2.5 per cent in 1960 to 1 per cent today; in Africa it remains high at 2 per cent. It is also worth noting that regional figures cover large differences between countries and socio-economic groups.

All countries in the world are experiencing a transformation in the distribution of their populations by age. The demographic transition model was developed by analysing the changes in population experienced by various countries around the world. Frank Notestein, an American demographer, developed the demographic transition theory, thereafter taken further by C. P. Blacker into a theory that spells out five types of populations (diminishing, low stationary, early expanding, stationary and high). The theory is useful in enabling researchers and economists to develop models that explain how the transformation of the population can be instrumental in addressing economic and social challenges nationally and globally.

Figure 9.1 shows us the five types of populations and the transformation that leads from one type to another. It also explains the fluctuation of the birth rate, death rate and natural increase (Palgrave Macmillan Ltd, 2013).

The ability of countries to manage the type of population they have and the transition from one type of population to another generates their ability to benefit economically and address social challenges such as poverty.

The key question we aim to further explore refers to uncovering the contexts in which African countries are able to ensure such a transition. Our argument is that African countries are able to do so if, and only if, African societies are well understood and respected, basing population policies on existing cultural institutions, practices and values. It is local societies that when empowered to act can generate the solutions for shaping the type of population the respective countries may need in order to take the benefits of the demographic dividend. In order to exemplify how local practices are essential for achieving the demographic dividend, we explore the case study of the pastoral communities from the Horn of Africa. In particular, we will reflect on their governance and sociocultural practices.

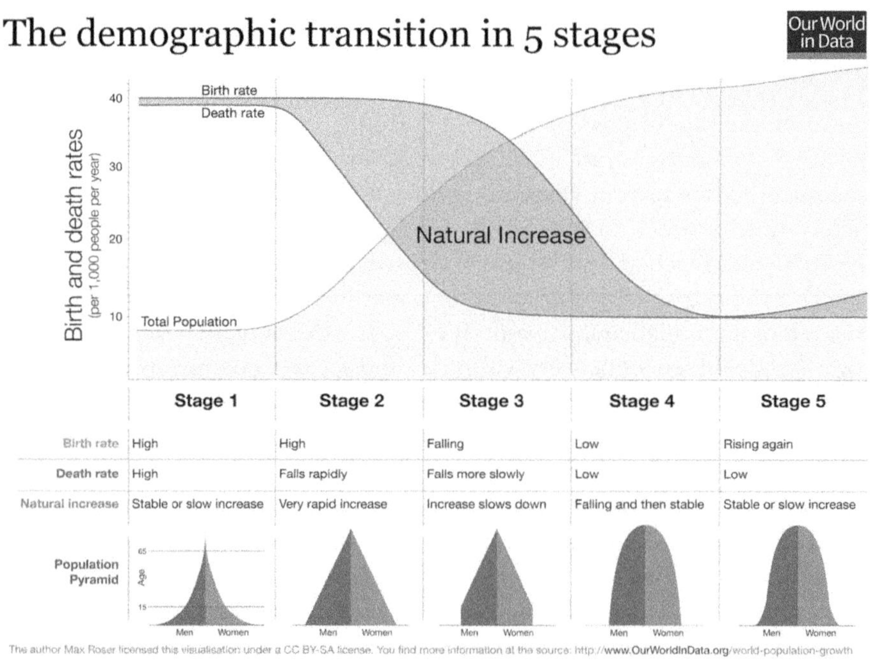

Figure 9.1 The five stages of the demographic transition.

Case Study: The Sociocultural Practices of Pastoral Communities in the Horn of Africa

Pastoralism refers to a lifestyle that relies on mobility and flexibility in the way land is utilised for ensuring a livelihood based on an extensive livestock production system. In the Horn of Africa, Ethiopia (60 per cent) as well as Djibouti, Somalia, Kenya and South Sudan encompass pastoral areas. In more specific terms, pastoral areas cover Afar and Somali regions, large areas of Southern Nations, Nationalities, and Peoples (SNNP) and Oromia regions, as well as parts of Gambella and Beneshangul-Gumuz, as illustrated in Figure 9.2 (Tefera et al., 2016).

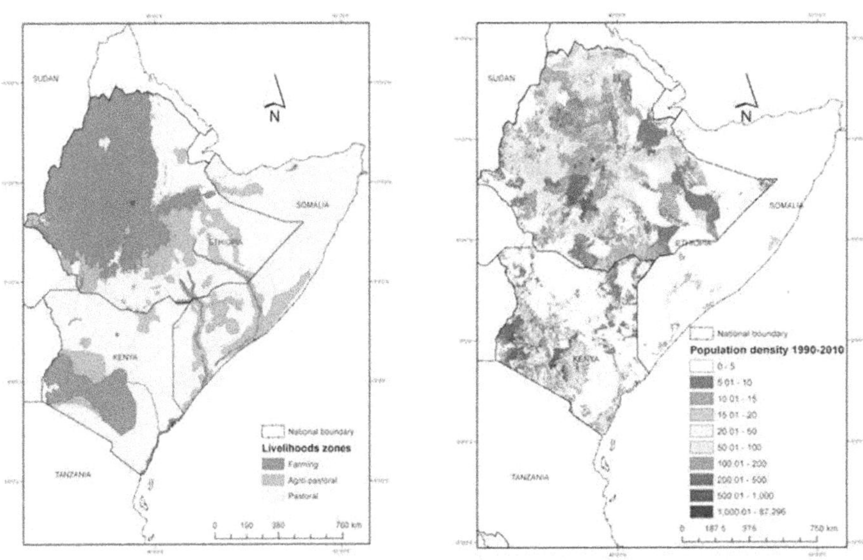

(a) (b)

Figure 9.2 (a) FEWS net livelihoods zones map for Ethiopia, Kenya and Somalia; (b) population density change map from 1990 to 2010.

Twenty-nine different ethnic groups, representing about 12 to 15 million of the Ethiopian population (90 million) were considered to lead an agro-pastoralist and pastoralist lifestyle in 2006 (MoFED, 2006). Their activity is carried out mostly in the drier lowland areas; however, there is also significant movement between the lowland and highland areas, for example, between Ale and Borana or between Amhara and Afar. The focus on livestock leads to a strong connection between the communities in these areas, both within country boundaries and in the broader region. That generates an economy of approximately US$50 million per year in Ethiopia alone, involving in 2015, an estimate of over 60 million livestock holdings (cattle, sheep, goats and camels) (Tefera et al., 2016).

Source: Pricope et al. (2013).

Pastoralism has historically ensured the sustainability of community livelihood in the Horn of Africa in a semi-arid environment. It relies on land tenure systems that are based on customary rules, generating customary institutions which played an important role in governing land, managing conflicts and protecting the environment. In the context of difficult environmental conditions, such arrangements were based on complex access and management rules and common property regimes. Given the above characteristics and the related cultural codes and practices, the pastoralist system was a complex adaptive system that ensured the sustainability of ecological and social systems for a long period of time. Despite the high number of communities involved (29), guiding governance principles were developed and shaped over time. They include, among others, a system of protection for group rights and assets, inclusivity, reciprocity and redistribution of assistance and wealth to poorer groups (Tefera et al., 2016).

There are usually clear, hierarchical governance structures that lead community decision-making processes. For example, among the Somali, who extend across Kenya, Somalia, Djibouti and Ethiopia, leadership is based on clans. The clan chief, called ugaas, plays a central role in political and administrative matters, prevention and resolution of conflicts and resource management. An ugaas, once elected, is in office for the duration of his life. While the sons and brothers of an ugaas can be considered for the role, the position is not hereditary. When an ugaas dies, a group of elders is established to select the new ugaas. In the governance hierarchy, below the ugaas is a leadership council of elders, representing the different sub-clans or houses within the clan (Tefera et al., 2016).

Another example of governance systems comes from the Oromo group (Boran, Arsi and Guji) which extends from Ethiopia into Kenya and Somalia. Here, social organisation is based on the Gada,

> a Boran age-grade or generation system in which one age-set rules for eight years in assuming political, military, judicial, legislative, and ritual responsibilities, before handing over to the next, younger age-set […]. At the head of the system, is the Abba gada composed of three selected leaders with different social and cultural responsibilities. The Gada system is complemented by the age-set system of Hariya. [...] All clans have a Hayyu (ritual leader or judge). (Tefera et al., 2016, p. 27)

They also have ritual priests (qallu), organisers of meetings (abba quaee) and messengers (jallaba). The clans rely on verbal decision-making processes and unwritten rules and regulations. Important to note is that the different customary institutions have certain prerogatives with regard to the use of land (Tefera et al., 2016).

These processes remained unseen or uncaptured by the Western conceptual frames underpinning development policies and existed as a shadow in between state policies in the region. 'The system survives into the 21st century, because it has not been forcibly extinguished by superimposed property systems, and because its community-based character allows ready adaption of norms as each generation finds necessary. This keeps it vibrant and relevant, including to changing land uses and social relations within the community' (Cotula, 2007). State legislation in the Horn of Africa failed to clearly define communal rights to rangelands and assign specific responsibilities and roles for communities and local government in ensuring the management of land resources. Such legal vacuums prevent pastoral communities from exercising their rights over land, lead to bypassing of traditional governance mechanisms and in consequence result in a significant destruction of the social, economic and environmental conditions of the region.

Ethiopia, with support from the Inter-Governmental Agency for Development (IGAD), as well as Kenya and Uganda, is attempting to regulate 'community landholdings' while enabling the aforementioned customary institutions to function. In Ethiopia, they are legally called 'Community Land Governance Entities – CLGE' and have a mandate to 'hold title to communal land, manage rangeland resources and represent the community in dealings with third parties, including the government and the private sector' (Tech, 2020). In Kenya, the Communal Land Act of 2016 enables the state to acknowledge customary tenure as producing lawful property rights, not merely rights of occupation and use on government or public lands. Other countries where community property governance processes have been adopted into state land management processes, including Uganda, Mozambique, Tanzania, South Sudan, Benin, Malawi, Mali and Burkina Faso. Ghana, Liberia, South Africa, Zambia and Namibia, have draft laws in hand. At least 10 other countries are working towards this objective, including Sierra Leone, Senegal, Morocco and the Democratic Republic of Congo.

This approach illustrates the ways in which communities work is increasingly being recognised. This comes after decades of development and consolidation of state rule over territories and populations that have had a sophisticated way of functioning. This lesson is to be highlighted as land use is not the only area where the wisdom, governance mechanisms and ways of life of local communities are ignored. As African countries have only a narrow window of opportunity to prepare and transform population growth in a population dividend, the lesson is significant. African societies expose a complex social environment which is little considered in approaches to population policies. Central aspects of social life, such as birth and death, relevance of children for families, responsibility of communities with regard to their development are all key dimensions of any social establishment. Our claim is that no population dividend is going to be arrived at without taking seriously the relevance of the practices of African societies.

Conclusion

In this short chapter, we present the inability of the international community, Western donors and, at times, African governments to recognise and understand the ways in which African societies work. Yet, it is often the case that exactly those invisible institutions generate the stability, peace, economic welfare and community strength needed for African societies to face the many challenges they are confronted with.

In the case of the pastoralist communities, we finally come to see, after several decades of alienating policies, that the customary institutions are offering solutions to complicated regional dynamics. Our proposition is that in regard to population policies, the international community, donors and African governments should not make the same mistake, given the implicated urgency and significant risks. It is African societies and communities that can bring a significant contribution to achieving the demographic dividend if they are finally accepted as a legitimate part of the process, given that it is their own future that development and population policies are, in effect, about.

However, African societies are diverse. In consequence, it is vital that the international community works to develop a minutiose understanding of local practices related to family relations, role of children and inheritance among others. Such an understanding would enable a proper identification of local actors and mechanisms embedded in local societies that can be engaged in developing local responses to the challenges that may impede the actualisation of the demographic dividend.

References

Acharya, A., Fuzzo de Lima, A. T., and Moore, M. 2006. 'Proliferation and Fragmentation: Transactions Costs and the Value of Aid'. *Journal of Development Studies*, 42, 11–21. https://www.tandfonline.com/doi/abs/10.1080/00220380500356225.

Alesina, A., and Dollar, D. 2000. 'Who Gives Foreign Aid to Whom and Why?' *Journal of Economic Growth*, 5, 33–63. https://link.springer.com/article/10.1023/A:1009874203400.

Alonso, J. A. 2012. *From Aid to Global Development Policy*. New York: DESA.

Berthélemy, J. C. 2006. 'Aid Allocation: Comparing Donors' Behaviors'. *Swedish Economic Policy Review*, 13, 75–109.

Burnside, C., and Dollar, D. 2000. 'Aid, Policies, and Growth'. *American Economic Review*, 847–68.

Cibian, S. 2011. *Analyzing the European Development Fund: An English School Account of How Presumed Statehood Undermines (Development in) Sub- Saharan Africa*. Budapest: Central European University.

Claessens, S., Cassimon, D., and van Camperhout, B. 2007. *Empirical Evidence on the New International Aid Architecture*. IMF.

Cotula, L. 2007. *Legal Empowerment for Local Resource Control: Securing Local Resource Rights within Foreign Investment Projects in Africa*. Hertfordshire, UK: Russell.

Dingwerth, K., and Pattberg, P. 2006. 'Global Governance as a Perspective on World Politics'. *Global Governance*, 185–203.

Headey, D. 2008. 'Geopolitics and the Effect of Foreign Aid on Economic Growth: 1970–2001'. *Journal of International Development*, 161–80.

Hoeffler, A., and Outram, V. 2011. 'Need, Merit, or Self Interest – What Determines the Allocation of Aid?' *Review of Development Economics*, 237–50.

Ibrahim, A. 2005. *HIV/AIDS, Gender and Reproductive Health Promotion: The Role of Traditional Institutions among the Borana Oromo, Southern Ethiopia*. Ethiopia: Finfinne.

Kanbur, R., and Sumner, A. 2012. 'Poor Countries or Poor People? Development Assistance and the New Geography of Global Poverty'. *Journal of International Development*, 686–95.

Kaul, I., Conceicao, P., Gouven, L. K., and Mendoza, R. U. 2003. *Providing Global Public Goods*. New York: Oxford University Press.

Kharas, H., and Rogerson, A. 2012. *Horizon 2025: Creative Destruction in the Aid Industry*. London: ODI.

Knack, S., and Rahman, A. 2008. *Donor Fragmentation*. Washington, DC: World Bank.

Lumsdaine, D. H. 1993. *Moral Vision in International Politics: The Foreign Aid Regime, 1949–1989*. Princeton, NJ: Princeton University Press.

Mawdsley, E., Savage, L., and Kim, S.-M. 2014. 'A "Post-Aid World"? Paradigm Shift in Foreign Aid and Development Cooperation at the 2011 Busan High Level Forum'. *Geographical Journal*, 27–38. https://rgs-ibg.onlinelibrary.wiley.com/doi/10.1111/j.1475-4959.2012.00490.x.

Migdal, J. S. 1988. *Strong Societies and Weak States: State-Society Relations and State Capabilities in the Third World*. Princeton, NJ: Princeton University Press.

MoFED. 2006. *Ethiopia: Building on Progress: A Plan for Accelerated and Sustained Development to End Poverty (PASDEP)*. Addis Ababa: Ministry of Finance and Economic Development.

Moyo, D. 2009. *Dead Aid: Why Aid Is Not Working and How There Is a Better Way for Africa*. New York: Farrar, Straus, and Giroux.

OECD. 2011. 'OECD Report on Division of Labour: Addressing Cross-Country Fragmentation of Aid'. 16 October. Retrieved from: http://www.oecd.org/dac/aid-architecture/49106391.pdf.

Palgrave Macmillan Ltd. 2013. 'International Historical Statistics'. P. M. Limited, Ed., April. Retrieved from: http://www.palgraveconnect.com/pc/doifinder/10.1057/9781137305688.

Petersen, A. 2011. *The World Island: Eurasian Geopolitics and the Fate of the West*. Santa Barbara, CA: Praeger.

Population Division, United Nations. 2016. World Population Prospects. 15 September. Retrieved from: https://population.un.org/wpp/DataQuery/.

Pricope, N., Husak, G., Lopez-Carr, D., Funk, C., and Michaelsen, J. 2013. 'The Climate-Population Nexus in the East African Horn: Emerging Degradation Trends in Rangeland and Pastoral Livelihood Zones'. *Global Environmental Change*, 23(6), 1525–41. https://www.sciencedirect.com/science/article/abs/pii/S0959378013001738.

Severino, J. M., and Ray, O. 2009. *The End of ODA: Death and Rebirth of a Global Public Policy*. Washington, DC: Center for Global Development.

———. 2010. *The End of ODA (II): The Birth of Hypercollective Action*. Washington, DC: Center for Global Development.

Sumner, A., and Mallett, R. 2013. *The Future of Foreign Aid: Development Cooperation and the New Geography of Poverty*. Houndmills: Palgrave Macmillan.

Tech, T. 2020. 'Formally Recognizing Pastoral Community Land Rights in Ethiopia'. 15 March. Retrieved from: https://landportal.org/blog-post/2018/04/formally-recognizing-pastoral-community-land-rights-ethiopia.

Tefera, D. A., Bijman, J., and Slingerland, M. A. 2016. 'Agricultural Co-operatives in Ethiopia: Evolution, Functions and Impact'. *Journal of International Development*. https://onlinelibrary.wiley.com/doi/full/10.1002/jid.3240.

Temple, J. 2010. 'Aid and Conditionality'. In D. Rodrik and M. Rosenzweig (eds), *Handbook of Development Economics*, vol. 5, pp. 4415–523. Oxford: Elsevier.

Worldometers. 2019. 'World Population Clock: 7.7 Billion People'. 27 April. Retrieved from: http://www.worldometers.info/world-population.

Chapter 10

REVISITING DEMOCRACY: INTERSECTIONALITY, YOUTH AND THE IMPERATIVE OF 'CLIMATE JUSTICE' – SARDINIA'S 'EUROPE DAY'

Colette Mazzucelli, Christian Rossi and Viola Prisca Roggia

Participation in Europe Day 2019 at the University of Cagliari is a case study that highlights the need to deepen the understanding of the youth about the implications of climate change on the society of an original European Union (EU) member state facing a crisis of democracy in the early twenty-first century. In this case, the focus is on the role of youth in Sardinia amidst the aging population in Italy, which is accompanied by high youth unemployment as well as immigration. Gender and race are specifically applicable in this narrative.

The effects of climate change on a natural disaster in Sardinia, along with the political and social response, are explained as part of an inquiry into the EU's strategy towards the young, aged 16–24. In this context, the younger segment in Italy's society is particularly vulnerable, in democratic terms, due to disinformation, populism and discrimination, as the EU is unsure about their impact on the youth. In order to harvest the demographic dividend, the negative impact of misinformation, demagoguery and inequity, which erodes trust in the institutions critical to the evolution of democracy in Italy, as well as Europe's fragile Union, must be increasingly countered with positive initiatives such as Europe Day 2019.

Europe Day 2019: Youth Participation at the University of Cagliari

Each year, European institutions, member states and universities across Europe celebrate Europe Day, which recalls the creation of the European Coal and

Steel Community on 9 May 1950. Europe Day 2019 at the University of Cagliari, which took place on 21 May 2019, focused on the engagement of Sardinia's oldest university, established in 1606, in the action schemes to promote cross-border cooperation and learning among the youth in the EU member states across the continent. Panels highlighted the impact of learning on Italian students in the context of Italy's participation in European integration, including a video project made by the students in communication at the University of Cagliari on the topic of 'Europe between Perception and Reality: The Strategic Value of Communication'. Universities across Europe, including Cagliari, are committed to the Bologna Process for Higher Education, in which the Lifelong Learning Project and the Youth Program figure prominently (Kooij, 2015; EC, 2020).

Looking ahead to a new decade, future Europe Day programmes in Sardinia and Italy may amplify themes presented in 2019, particularly those related to ecology and the environment (Brereton and O'Neill, 2019). The ruling by the Supreme Court of the Netherlands on 20 December 2019 has far-reaching implications for litigation across Europe and around the world. In its ruling, the Supreme Court mandated the government of the Netherlands to reduce emissions by at least 25 per cent by the end of 2020, as compared to 1990s levels, reaching well beyond the EU-wide objective of 20 per cent (Dunn, 2019). This ruling is one that speaks to the younger generations whose lives are most likely to be influenced in the decades to come by climate change.

In terms of societal engagement, the Supreme Court ruling provides the basis for a transnational youth movement, which advocates for increased emission reductions by governments as a human right. It is a law with the potential to leverage the youth dividend in Sardinia, Italy, Europe and other parts of the world, by focusing the attention of the younger generations during their university studies on the imperative to respect the environment to prevent a planetary catastrophe (Smith et al., 2019).

This youth movement in support of transnational engagement, which may anchor the Netherlands' Supreme Court ruling in the daily lives of Italian and European citizens, is one that could aim to champion what is defined by Mazzucelli (2020) as 'intersectional diplomacy', representing the interests of the future generations whose lives are most threatened by climate change, on the basis of inclusivity, thereby bearing in mind that human needs, in this context, cannot be denied along class, gender or race lines.

Youth in the European Union: Italy and Sardinia in Context

The EU has long been committed to designing a Strategy for Young People, which has been codified in the Treaty on the Functioning of the European

Union (TFEU, 2012). The definition of 'young people' differs across Europe according to period, socio-economic development and national context (EC, 2018a). A strategy for young European citizens was also inserted into the Bologna Process for Higher Education. Starting in 2013, the European Commission designed a framework for cooperation in the field of youth, whose primary objective was to enhance the participation of younger generations in democratic life and society. The intent of the 2013 strategy was to inspire young voters and urge their generation to participate in the 2014 European elections. For this reason, the European Commission ordered a survey designed to understand the attitudes of people, aged 15–30. The survey was created following the 2010 EU Youth Strategy (EC, 2018c). It was concentrated on youngsters' involvement in sports groups, youth and cultural organisations, participation in political elections at different levels, checking their awareness and possible participation in the European elections, trying to predict the predisposition to vote and their expectations (EC, 2013).

The strategy was revised in 2018 after a long-term assessment by the European Commission concluded with a report that evaluated the progress made towards the overall objectives of the framework strategy itself, highlighting the novelty of the main trends already selected and identifying good practices for the subsequent strategy. The EU report tried to cover all the EU member states as well as candidate countries and the European Economic Area (EEA) countries. These main trends are all connected; it is important that they are developed in synergy. The most important appears to be the boost for young people's higher level of education and their interest in politics and participation in democratic life due to the possibilities offered by new technologies.

With respect to education, the commission noted the increase of all trends, particularly the upper secondary level, including higher degrees. Political life participation seems strictly linked to the improved opportunities in education, employment and subsequent progress in social inclusion, all factors that contribute to reviving the young generation's interest in political and civic issues, inspiring them to re-engage with society. New technologies, the internet and greater availability of social media helped the development of this renewed attention shown by the young generation for political issues (EC, 2018a). If, on the one hand, this new political revival is strategic for the EU and for democracy, on the other hand, it seems important to be vigilant in order to check that the youngsters are provided with true and genuine information. In this way, the youth do not receive a distorted perception of reality through the expansion of disinformation campaigns, which are a threat to democracy (EC, 2018d).

The erosion of democracy proved to be the most alarming trend for the European Commission as the electoral turnout of young people has drastically declined over the years, particularly in the European elections. The democratic participation is also linked to persisting inequalities, particularly between genders. The commission, in its report, also highlighted the fact that there is still a geographical gap among Western, Southern, and Eastern Europe, as these last two regions face higher challenges in terms of education, employment, inclusion and the use of digital technologies, noting that this fact has an impact in terms of democratic participation (EC, 2018a).

According to the European Commission's studies, young people need to take back control of their lives and participate with renewed engagement in civil society. Their future is threatened by climate change as well as by demographic trends, social exclusion and discrimination. All these are phenomena that have an indefinite impact on the job market and on the democratic process. Young people must prove to be resilient and adapt to this unprecedented situation in which they are at risk of finding themselves in an increasingly worsening economic situation with respect to their parents. It is important to highlight that 11.6 per cent of young people between the ages of 16 and 24 years are neither working nor pursuing an educational path. Socio-economic exclusion means democratic self-exclusion (EC, 2017). The EU is obviously concerned about this phenomenon, as people in that situation are normally less active as citizens with a distrust for institutions and with less mobility abroad. The principal aim of the EU Strategy for Young People is to make the youth responsible for their future and the future of the environment where they live (Soltes et al., 2020). This strategy will be accomplished through three main steps: mobilising, connecting and increasing responsibility. The universities of Europe can play a part if they are successful in creating more linkages across borders and by encouraging students to increase their Erasmus+ experiences (EC, 2018b).

Universities in Italy, particularly those in frontier locations, such as Sardinia, are working to build a network that leads students to increase their knowledge with broad access to all the resources of the planned consortium (General Secretariat of the Council, 2017). The university system can thus be a stimulus for a greater use of digital technology as well as a place to bring attention to the sustainability of the ecosystem in the wake of climate change, as recalled by the United Nations on the occasion of the adoption of the 2030 Agenda for Sustainable Development in 2015 (Kabanbayeva et al., 2019).

The agenda connects perfectly to the European Strategy for Youth with many points in common. The UN expressed concern about the difficult sustainability of the present environmental, economic and social development model inviting civil society and its institutions to define a new strategy of sustainability, which can help in reaching the UN's objectives by 2030 (UN General Assembly, 2015). Climate change and sustainability are two fields in which the university can play a pivotal role for the future. Sardinia, as a case study, is one of the peripheral regions of Italy that has been deeply affected over the past 20 years by climate change (Satta, 2020), which, since the past five years, is now perceived by the general population and not only by experts as the invasion of locusts during summer 2019 illustrates, as well as the intensive floods the island has experienced. This is a problem also highlighted by the president of the Region of Sardinia during a meeting of the Committee of the Regions in Brussels in 2018 (European Committee of the Regions, 2018).

Overcoming Intergenerational Discrimination to Harvest the Demographic Dividend

The relationship between adults and young people has emerged as being problematic on several occasions in the Italian society. Generally, adult attitudes seem to exude scepticism and suspicion because of their lack of understanding of younger generations. These attitudes seem to be at times mixed with a sense of nostalgia for their own youth. Furthermore, adult attitudes may be exacerbated by their uncomfortable position resulting from being trapped between an older generation that is living increasingly longer and a younger generation that relies on their older counterparts financially, especially during college or graduate education.

The adult generation's criticism of younger individuals emerge when they seem to recall nostalgically the student uprising in which they participated during the 1970s and 1980s, while looking down on younger people's environmental protests. The adults claim that the 1970s protests promoted actual ideals and had solid ideological foundations whereas current protests are guided by youth willingness to avoid class or weak demands, at best. However, youth motivations resemble the ones driving students 50 years ago: a compromise between the willingness to be subversive typical of the youth and the desire to skip class. In other words, young people decided to join these protests for several reasons – exactly like events that happened 50 years ago (Gallizioli, 2019).

Different motivations result in different kinds of mobilisation, as the environmental cause has touched young people on different levels. For example, embracing the environmental cause awakened ecological awareness in a lot of young people. This, in turn, transformed their consumption and everyday life choices. Some started asking for recycling bins in the classrooms. Some started filling their water bottles and boycotting the vending machines that offer only plastic water bottles. Some requested teachers to turn off the lights in the classrooms that are not in use. Some others started making more radical choices, such as travelling to school by public transportation rather than by car or moped. Some stopped printing hard copies and used only digital versions of documents. Others asked their principals to avoid turning on the heating system right at the beginning of fall. Hence, the environmental cause and protests made young people change their behaviours; the youth thus became protagonists in their active choices.

Furthermore, the environmental cause set in motion deeper thinking in some young people. Some began to realise that only a global effort will produce an effective response to climate change. Others realised that their choices affect other people and their planet as well as their own lives, and, consequently, started consciously to think about their future. These might be small steps in terms of an effective response to climate change. However, developing an ecological awareness is a fundamental precondition for young people to continue along this path, which might translate into a life of more ecologically friendly choices or even more ambitious projects (Gallizioli, 2019).

An example of an ambitious young Italian woman is Federica Gasbarro. This 24-year-old biology student was the only Italian participating in the Climate Action Summit 2019 at the UN in New York. She submitted her proposal project to the UN initiative to fight climate change, along with 99 other proposals. Federica had a positive impression, which motivated her to continue pursuing the environmental cause. Currently, she is working on a book addressing climate change (Mistretta, 2019).

The enthusiasm generated by the environmental cause might give younger generations the chance to energise their awareness and active roles in areas that do not strictly concern the fight against climate change. For instance, this might be an opportunity to counter the racist and unsympathetic hatred, which is poisoning Italian popular culture, incited by populist leaders. Young people's critical thinking and activism might allow them to go beyond a pessimistic and resigned attitude towards promoting positivity and optimism. However, older generations seem determined to hamper young people's enthusiasm. This determination seems apparent in the traditional media, which in Italy often dismiss and ridicule young people, who are not given a lot of space and are often reduced to stereotypes of naïve and ignorant people (Dondi, 2019). The young generation's obstacles seem compounded as young people are a smaller fraction of the Italian population compared to the elderly, particularly in Sardinia (see Table 10.1; ISTAT, 2019a).

However, young people have at their disposal technological means, the understanding of which is lacking among many adults. Although one might argue that such means created greater, yet shallower, connections, these wider and global networks can be used for social mobilisation and promoting activism.

Table 10.1 Resident population by age

Italy				Sardinia			
Age	**Male (%)**	**Female (%)**	**Total (%)**	**Age**	**Male (%)**	**Female (%)**	**Total (%)**
0–4	1,216,600 (51.40)	1,151,086 (48.60)	2,367,686 (3.90)	0–4	27,114 (51.80)	25,207 (48.20)	52,321 (3.20)
5–9	1,400,494 (51.40)	1,322,302 (48.60)	2,722,796 (4.50)	5–9	33,119 (51.80)	30,868 (48.20)	63,987 (3.90)
10–14	1,478,693 (51.50)	1,393,040 (48.50)	2,871,733 (4.80)	10–14	34,890 (51.70)	32,603 (48.30)	67,493 (4.10)
15–19	1,501,907 (51.80)	1,395,234 (48.20)	2,897,141 (4.80)	15–19	36,848 (52.10)	33,898 (47.90)	70,746 (4.30)
20–24	1,567,021 (52.40)	1,423,224 (47.60)	2,990,245 (5.00)	20–24	39,623 (53.40)	34,509 (46.60)	74,132 (4.50)
25–29	1,645,183 (51.20)	1,565,842 (48.80)	3,211,025 (5.30)	25–29	43,871 (52.00)	40,530 (48.00)	84,401 (5.10)
30–34	1,701,202 (50.50)	1,668,144 (49.50)	3,369,346 (5.60)	30–34	46,598 (51.30)	44,205 (48.70)	90,803 (5.50)
35–39	1,857,949 (50.10)	1,846,923 (49.90)	3,704,872 (6.10)	35–39	52,206 (50.80)	50,514 (49.20)	102,720 (6.30)
40–44	2,203,460 (49.90)	2,214,897 (50.10)	4,418,357 (7.30)	40–44	63,778 (50.90)	61,479 (49.10)	125,257 (7.60)
45–49	2,390,329 (49.50)	2,433,968 (50.50)	4,824,297 (8.00)	45–49	67,745 (50.20)	67,125 (49.80)	134,870 (8.20)
50–54	2,430,424 (49.30)	2,503,912 (50.70)	4,934,336 (8.20)	50–54	68,239 (49.50)	69,487 (50.50)	137,726 (8.40)

(continued)

Table 10.1 *(cont.)*

Italy				**Sardinia**			
Age	**Male (%)**	**Female (%)**	**Total (%)**	**Age**	**Male (%)**	**Female (%)**	**Total (%)**
55–59	2,148,186 (48.60)	2,269,709 (51.40)	4,417,895 (7.30)	55–59	62,770 (48.90)	65,654 (51.10)	128,424 (7.80)
60–64	1,848,434 (48.10)	1,997,803 (51.90)	3,846,237 (6.40)	60–64	56,843 (48.50)	60,254 (51.50)	117,097 (7.10)
65–69	1,662,603 (47.60)	1,828,370 (52.40)	3,490,973 (5.80)	65–69	51,240 (48.40)	54,717 (51.60)	105,957 (6.50)
70–74	1,511,424 (46.70)	1,722,428 (53.30)	3,233,852 (5.40)	70–74	43,863 (47.40)	48,689 (52.60)	92,552 (5.60)
75–79	1,215,576 (44.50)	1,513,105 (55.50)	2,728,681 (4.50)	75–79	34,467 (44.40)	43,192 (55.60)	77,659 (4.70)
80–84	900,445 (41.40)	1,276,137 (58.60)	2,176,582 (3.60)	80–84	23,162 (41.10)	33,189 (58.90)	56,351 (3.40)
85–89	495,508 (35.90)	883,456 (64.10)	1,378,964 (2.30)	85–89	13,427 (36.60)	23,223 (63.40)	36,650 (2.20)
90–94	173,064 (28.60)	432,500 (71.40)	605,564 (1.00)	90–94	4,801 (29.90)	11,231 (70.10)	16,032 (1.00)
95–99	33,940 (22.00)	120,568 (78.00)	154,508 (0.30)	95–99	1,068 (26.70)	2,933 (73.30)	4,001 (0.20)
100+	2,324 (16.10)	12,132 (83.90)	14,456 (0.00)	100+	90 (21.80)	322 (78.20)	412 (0.00)
Total	29,384,766 (48.70)	30,974,780 (51.30)	60,359,546 (100)	Total	805,762 (49.10)	833,829 (50.90)	1,639,591 (100)

In conclusion, Europe Day 2019, as has occurred in the past, can be seen as a time for reflection about what has been achieved and as a motivation for action in the future. The programme of Europe Day focused on themes that speak to Italy's role in European integration. Yet, in order to harvest the demographic dividend, it is imperative to add panels addressing climate change and gender exclusion to stimulate the imaginations and motivate young people to engage more readily to address these local, regional, national, European and global concerns. Europe Day in Sardinia can evolve to tap into the European Commission's studies, cited earlier in this chapter, to support young people, which in Italy is necessary to counter the intergenerational strife that is a subject of this analysis.

The Europe Day programme can be designed to respond more to the needs of youth who face tremendous uncertainty given the unemployment among the young in Italy, which exacerbates the social exclusion of those of a certain generational experience. Given the threat of climate change looking ahead to the future of the younger generations, their engagement on behalf of the health of the planet can enhance their democratic participation as well in an era when disinformation deepens their mistrust of established institutions. More initiatives like Europe Day must engage the youth so that the EU Strategy for Young People is realised, thereby inspiring the youth to take responsibility for their future and the future of the environment they inhabit. The challenge the universities of Italy face is one of mobilisation to harvest the demographic dividend as the national population ages. Their role must evolve as a catalyst of youth participation in the democratic life of the Italian society as well as a transnational youth movement in the context of Europe's integration, which requires deeper linkages across borders supported by the intercultural awareness nurtured by exchange programs.

References

Brereton, Finbarr, and O'Neill, Eoin. 2019. 'Europe in Transition: The Future Place of the Environment in the European Union'. *Economic & Social Review*, Autumn, vol. 50, issue 3.

Dondi, Beatrice. 2019. *Il sistematico (e vendicativo) fastidio della tv nei confronti dei ragazzi, L'Espresso*. 21 October.

Dunn, Katherine. 2019. 'Climate Change Litigation Enters a New Era as Court Rules That Emissions Reduction Is a Human Right'. *Fortune*, 20 December. https://fortune.com/2019 /12/20/climate-change-litigation-human-rights-netherlands/.

EC (European Commission). 2013. 'European Youth: Participation in Democratic Life'. *Flash Euro-Barometer* 375, Report, May.

———. 2018a. 'Situation of Young People in the European Union'. Commission Staff Working Document 169, 22 May.

———. 2018b. 'Communication from the Commission to the European Parliament, the European Council, the Council, the European Economic and Social Committee and the Committee of the Regions – Engaging, Connecting and Empowering Young People: A New EU Youth Strategy'. COM 269, 22 May.

———. 2018c. *EU Youth Strategy 2010–2018*. https://ec.europa.eu/youth/policy/youth-strategy /strategy-2010-2018_en.

———. 2018d. 'Joint Communication to the European Parliament, the European Council, the Council, the European Economic and Social Committee and the Committee of the Regions, Action Plan against Disinformation 36'. 5 December.

———. 2020. 'The Bologna Process and the European Higher Education Area'. https://ec.europa.eu/education/policies/higher-education/bologna-process-and-european-higher-education-area_en.

European Committee of the Regions. 2018. 'Sardinia Reflects on Europe and Climate Change'. EU's Assembly of Regional and Local Representatives, 22 May. https://cor.europa.eu/en/news/ Pages/Sardinia-reflects-on-Europe-and-climate-change.aspx.

Gallizioli, Marco. 2019. 'L'onda verde giovanile'. *Rocca* 21, 1 November, 40–42.

General Secretariat of the Council. 2017. 'European Council Meeting – Conclusions'. European Council CO EUR 24 CONCL 7, 14 December. https://www.consilium.europa.eu /media/32204/14-final-conclusions-rev1-en.pdf.

Istituto Nazionale di Statistica (ISTAT). 2019a. 'Popolazione residente al 1° gennaio 2019 per fascia d'età – Italia'. http://dati.istat.it/Index.aspx?QueryId=18975.

———. 2019b. 'Popolazione residente al 1° gennaio 2019 per fascia d'età – Sardegna'. http://dati.istat.it/Index.aspx?QueryId=18975.

Kabanbayeva, Gulbakyt, Gureva, Maria, Bielik, Peter, and Ostasz, Grzegorz. 2019. 'Academic Mobility and Financial Stability: A Case of Erasmus Student Exchange Program'. *Journal of International Studies*, vol. 12, issue 1.

Kooij, Yasemin. 2015. *European Higher Education Policy and the Social Dimension: A Comparative Study of the Bologna Process*. Basingstoke: Palgrave Macmillan.

Mazzucelli, Colette. 2020. *Intersectional Diplomacy: Variations in LEAD Time*. Unpublished essay.

Mistretta, Mariangela. 2019. 'La nostra voce per il clima'. *D di Repubblica*, 26 October, 41–42.

Satta, Alessio. 2020. 'Climate Change – Integrated Coastal Zone Management'. Sardegna Coste, Regione Autonoma della Sardegna. http://www.sardegnaambiente.it/index.php?xsl=1809&s=23 &v=9&c=9514&es=4272&na=1&n=10&l=2.

Smith, Don C., Banet, Catherine, and Romera, Beatriz Martinez. 2019. 'Teaching the Law of Energy Transition in the Era of Internationalisation and Digitalisation of Legal University Education: The Transatlantic University Collaboration in Climate Change and Energy Law (TUCCCEL) Programme'. *Journal of Energy & Natural Resources Law*, vol. 37, issue 4, 455–64.

Soltes, Erik, Vojtkova, Maria, and Soltesova, Tatiana. 2020. 'Changes in the Geographical Distribution of Youth Poverty and Social Exclusion in EU Member Countries between 2008 and 2017'. *Moravian Geographical Reports*, vol. 28, issue 1, 2–10.

TFEU. 2012. 'Consolidated Version of the Treaty on the Functioning of the European Union'. *Official Journal of the European Union* C 326/47, art. 165. https://eur-lex.europa.eu/legal-content/EN/TXT/?uri=celex%3A12012E%2FTXT.

United Nations General Assembly. 2015. 'Resolution Adopted by the General Assembly on 25 September 2015 – Transforming Our World: The 2030 Agenda for Sustainable Development'. Resolution A/RES/70/1, 21 October. https://www.un.org/ga/search/view_doc.asp?symbol=A/RES/70/1&Lang=E.

ACKNOWLEDGEMENTS

This book has been a team effort and is the product of two labs, held under the aegis of the Global Diplomacy Lab (GDL) in Accra, Ghana, in June 2019 and in Berlin, Germany, in December 2019 on the topic 'Global Power Shifts: Political and Economic Inclusion for the Next Generation Collaborating to Realise the Potential of the Demographic Dividend'.

We would like to thank the Secretariat and leading partners of the GDL for placing their trust in us and supporting this project. In particular, we would like to thank Senta Hoefer, our faithful guide and mentor. Several GDL members are contributors and collaborators. Prof. Colette Mazzucelli of NYU Steinhardt has been extremely helpful in introducing us to Anthem Press for this publication. She also co-wrote a chapter.

We would like to thank all the contributing authors who gave of their time and expertise to this project, working with us across different time zones and on short deadlines: Stefan Cibian, Rudrani Dasgupta, Lynn Houmdi, Kebba-Omar Jagne, Julia Jaroschewski, Elizabeth Maloba, Patrick Mpedzisi, Viola Prisca Roggia, Christian Rossi, Annegret Warth and Ekua Yankah.

We would like to thank Anne-Christine Keienburg and Dr. Wiebke Koenig of the Global Leadership Academy under the GIZ (the German technical cooperation agency), and Stella Pfisterer of Erasmus University's Rotterdam School of Management who were quick to connect us with experts who did the peer review exercise. We are grateful to the following peer reviewers: Elizabeth Adekunle, Prof. Fidelis Allen, Marije Balt, Laila Bouallouch, Melanie Cheary, Yannick du Pont, Vijitha Mahadevan Eyango, Fabrice Fifonsi, Stephen Hunt, Dr. Manjunath Sadashiva, Natalia Sanchez, Dr. Geci Karuri Sebina, Mark Snijder, Henri Stetter, Dr. Annapurna Vancheswaran and Prof. Liane Woerner.

We would like to thank Julie August for the beautiful cover design for the compendium.

Last, we, the editors, are in deep agreement that it has been such a pleasure working together on this compendium. It has been truly a labour of love, and we have had much to gain from it. We would like to express our deep appreciation to our partners, family and friends who have supported us on this journey.

INDEX

Lightning Source UK Ltd.
Milton Keynes UK
UKHW041519061021
391728UK00001B/18

9 781785 276316